ARE WE AFRAID OF OUR CHILDREN?

When our children say "No!" to us, do we ask ourselves, "What did I do wrong?" Do we run to check the experts who can tell us, word for word, what to say? Too many parents feel uncertain of themselves, afraid and guilty, says Mrs. Eda LeShan. In Natural Parenthood, she advocates a return to self-confidence: raising children "from the heart"; growing, thinking, and learning ourselves and applying that knowledge to helping our children fulfill themselves.

These are the fresh, sensible, unorthodox views of a psychologist whose commentary is heard on National Educational TV, whose articles appear in magazines such as the New York Times Sunday Magazine, Parents *and* McCall's, *and whose books include* How to Survive Parenthood, Sex and Your Teen Ager *and* The Conspiracy Against Childhood. *Learn what she thinks about telling small-fry about war, the parents' responsibility in preventing homosexuality, working mothers, choosing a therapist, and even your inalienable right to raise your child without a script.*

Other SIGNET Books You Will Enjoy

Natural Parenthood:

Raising Your Child without a Script

by Eda LeShan

A SIGNET BOOK from
NEW AMERICAN LIBRARY
TIMES MIRROR

This book is gratefully dedicated to the Eastern Educational Television Station in New York City and to its program *Newsfront*, which provided me with an opportunity to present these commentaries. My special thanks to Lee Hayes, Mitchell Krause, and Lee Polk.

Acknowledgments

"Children and Chores" originally appeared as "The Chore War," *Redbook* magazine, March, 1968.

"Sibling Rivalry Is Here To Stay" originally appeared as "Brotherly—Love" in *The New York Times Magazine*, November 22, 1964. © 1964 by The New York Times Company. Reprinted by permission.

"The Man in Your Daughter's Life" originally appeared as "The Man in Her Life" in *The New York Times Magazine*, August 15, 1965. © 1965 by The New York Times Company. Reprinted by permission.

"Social Life in the Grades" is reprinted from the March 1965 issue of *The PTA Magazine* by permission.

"Healthy and Irritating Signs of Independence" is reprinted from the February 1960 issue of *The PTA Magazine* by permission.

"The Under-Deprived Child" originally appeared in *The New York Times Magazine*, April 13, 1966. © 1966 by The New York Times Company. Reprinted by permission.

"The Teen-Ager and the Telephone" is reprinted by Permission of *McCall's*.

"Are We Afraid of Our Children?" originally appeared as "Are You Afraid of Your Children?" and is reprinted from the December 1967 issue of *The PTA Magazine* by permission.

"The Care and Feeding of Parents" originally appeared as "A Dr. Spock for Parents" in *The New York Times Magazine*, August 28, 1966. © 1966 by The New York Times Company. Reprinted by permission.

The balance of this book consists of commentaries originally presented by Mrs. LeShan on Newsfront, Channel 13/WNDT during the period 1968 to 1969.

(The following page constitutes an extension of this copyright page.)

SIGNET, SIGNET CLASSICS, MENTOR, PLUME AND MERIDIAN BOOKS
are published by The New American Library, Inc.,
1301 Avenue of the Americas, New York, New York 10019

FIRST SIGNET PRINTING, MARCH, 1970

7 8 9 10 11 12 13 14

PRINTED IN THE UNITED STATES OF AMERICA

CONTENTS

Section III   111

Section IV   147

INTRODUCTION

We have now had about fifty years of scientific scrutiny of child-raising methods, and it is beginning to occur to some of us who have been involved in some part of this that few of the expectations with which this era of child study began have been realized. It's a discouraging thought!

The truth of the matter seems to be that there is *more* confusion and *more* conflict about what is "right" or "wrong" in child-raising procedures. Rather than having discovered some useful eternal verities, we have, from decade to decade, swung wildly from one extreme to another until parent and expert alike are breathless and dizzy. A survey in *The Ladies Home Journal* reported that the majority of today's parents are "retreating on almost all fronts"—that they are confused, even panic-stricken, that they are afraid of their children and of losing their love and approval, afraid their children will turn against them. The report said, "Many parents feel so guilty about their own shortcomings that they appear incapable of straightening out their children. Many parents are so tyrannized by their children that they are not altogether sure that adults are still running the world."

It would seem, indeed, that rather than being made wiser and stronger by information provided by psychiatrists, psychologists, social workers, and educators, many parents have become so immobilized that a new brand of expert seems to be coming to the conclusion that 1) parents must be given specific lesson plans for raising children, or 2) they simply can't be relied on at all! The first category is well represented by Dr. Haim Ginott and his bestseller, *Between Parent and Child*. He offers today's confused and frightened parent a very well-written script for what to say to his child under every possible circumstance; little is left to chance or imagination. The second approach gives up on parents altogether; parenthood is seen as simply too difficult and complicated to leave to untrained, ordinary human beings! Harvard psychologist B. F. Skinner writes, "I despair of teaching the ordinary parent how to handle his child. I would prefer to turn child-raising over to a specialist. I just can't believe that an ordinary parent can do a good job." A psychologist at Cornell University was recently quoted (in *Today's Child*, January, 1968) as saying, "There is no quality control over parenthood. We already regulate things like who can drive and who can teach—why not parenthood?" He went on to say that only people who are competent should have children and that social scientists should be the ones to decide who is qualified. They should also provide the training for couples who flunk out as prospective parents. "Until they pass the test, no children."

Assuming that this solution may seem attractive to the more bewildered and disillusioned among us, where do we find those social scientists who can straighten it all out? The generally accepted observation that the children of psychiatrists, psychologists, and other social scientists hardly seem to represent this sought-after goal of human perfection was further verified by an article in *Redbook* Magazine (January, 1968) by Dr. Daniel Malamud, entitled "Do Psychologists Make Good Parents?" Dr. Malamud met in a discussion on parenthood with five couples in which either husband or wife or both were professional psychotherapists. He reported that "therapists don't differ very much at all from other parents. We're faced with all the typical parent's dilemmas—and we often react with anger or jealousy or embarrassment."

It would seem that parents are now faced with the choice of letting their children be raised, robotlike, by rules and laws handed down from some still undefined "higher authority" or of just going on muddling-through as ordinary people (psychotherapists apparently included) doing the best they can, using what information they can garner in conjunction with their own feelings and instincts: using whatever wisdom and common sense they have, is what it amounts to. Maybe that, and good will and love, are all we've got going for us.

My own conclusion is that human beings, being human, have refused all along to be categorized, and that children, perhaps most of all, tend to be rugged individualists, not easily influenced by *any* theory or *any* formula. I am inclined to be comforted by, and agree with, Dr. Malamud, who concluded, "There seems to be little doubt that the parent who can accept the fact that he can make errors, yet still be a good parent, helps his child to see that *he too* can be less than perfect, and still be a good person."

It seems to me that we *do* have a choice to make—a very crucial one. In this age of technology, of mechanization and machine-worship, of pseudo-science, I suppose that sooner or later we could invent a mechanical parent run by a no-mistakes computer. But we can be certain that the children raised by this science-fiction monster would be mechanical children. For myself, I choose the imperfect human—the parent who struggles throughout his life to become most himself, who searches for his unique strengths, who lets himself experience life most fully—both its anguish and its joys. Parenthood without a script, in other words.

In his brilliant and important book *Toward a Psychology of Being,** Dr. Abraham Maslow, former President of The American Psychological Association, wrote, "Every age but ours has had its model, its ideal. All these have been given up by our culture; the saint, the hero, the gentleman, the knight, the mystic. About all we have left is the well adjusted man without problems, a very pale substitute. Perhaps we shall soon be able to use as our guide and model the fully growing and self-fulfilling human being, the one whose inner nature expresses itself freely, rather than being warped, suppressed or denied."

Some people seem to misunderstand what it means to set a goal of this kind. They get the mistaken notion that just about anybody can raise a "fully growing and self-fulfilling human being"—after all, there don't seem to be

* Princeton, N.J.: Van Nostrand, 1962.

any absolute rules, it's all kind of vague. Once, in a parent discussion group when we were discussing the difference between rigid theories for parents and the encouragement of individual spontaneity, a mother said to me, "Aren't you advocating a sort of 'Natural Parenthood' where a parent just does whatever comes naturally?"

Perhaps I can clarify this question by comparing it to the parallel case of Natural Childbirth. Certainly its proponents believe that birth is a natural phenomenon! But in spite of that fact they provide extensive training programs and encourage parents to approach the birth of their child in a disciplined and knowledgeable way; there is nothing laissez-faire about their procedures. At the same time, no two couples who have been trained in Natural Childbirth classes are ever expected to have the same kind of experience—or to react in exactly the same ways as any other couple. Uniqueness, individual needs and differences, a sense of wonder and newness, are seen as essential and profoundly significant parts of the experience.

If I thought that parents should just do "whatever comes naturally," I wouldn't have knocked myself out for more than twenty-five years talking to parents' groups, writing articles and books, and speaking on television. Over the past half-century we *have* been accumulating a useful and important body of knowledge about how children grow—how they feel, what they need, what helps them to grow well. In the course of this development we have made a great many errors, we have gone off half-cocked on many issues; trial and error are inevitable in human progress. But it seems to me that it does help a parent a great deal to know as much as he can about children and child raising—to be as informed as he can be about human growth and development.

Being an informed parent seems to me to mean trying to know as much about as many things as one can. Whatever ways we find that suit us best to go on growing and thinking and learning are bound to enrich what we bring to parenthood. I have never suggested that knowledge wasn't important or that broadening one's life experiences wasn't constructive and helpful in child raising.

The fundamental question of Natural Parenthood is what a parent does with what he learns. Does he make a religion out of one book or a God of one expert? Does he look for final answers, for comfortable formulas? Does he search for some panacea for solving problems, refusing to acknowledge that problems are part of the nature of growing?

It seems to me that being a "natural parent" also means striving to become a better, wiser, more sensitive human being, but always accepting the fact of that humanness: acknowledging one's uniqueness, one's own special needs and ways, taking pride in one's ability to make one's own judgments, and accepting the fact that if one is human, one will *always* have problems, one will *always* experience frustration and pain as well as exultancy and joy.

In Natural Parenthood you never know any final answers; the answers you find, change as you and your child change, and are adapted to your very special personalities. You also never expect or want life to be easy or uncomplicated; you accept the fact that the struggle to be most deeply and truly alive is never-ending and never easy. And when you read books like this one, you take from it what seems to make sense—if it does—and adapt it to your particular situation and needs, rejecting whatever seems foolish or just plain wrong. I respect each of you enough to "tell it like I see it," trusting you to challenge me. I expect you to understand that I can only offer what I think I've learned so far, but that, along with you, I plan to go on changing and growing all of my life. That's the one real gift we have to give to our children—our openness to experience, our ability to grow.

For those of us who choose to struggle along with our humanness, Aldous Huxley said, "To aspire to be superhuman is a most discreditable admission that you lack the guts, the wit, the moderating judgment, to be successfully and consumately human."

SECTION
I

The Spoiled Child

About the worst thing anybody can say about a child is that he's "spoiled," but there is considerable confusion about what this means. The "spoiled child" is usually a child who has been given too much of the wrong things and not enough of the right things. It is an unfortunate expression because as commonly used it has taken on the connotation of an unpleasant, rude, unfriendly, irresponsible child who "has too much of everything." When someone describes a child as "spoiled," the almost universal reaction is to think of a child who has too many toys and other material possessions, too many privileges, too much freedom. In one sense this may be correct, for that is often what we see on the surface. What we don't see, but what is far more important, is that such a child *doesn't* have the guidance, the controls, the opportunity for developing his inner resources, the security of adult supervision and attention—the things which mean genuine love and security in a child's life. The spoiled child is actually a severely deprived child. It is the missing ingredients that make us dislike him and make him dislike himself, and his behavior can more accurately be judged as that of an unhappy, uncertain child, deprived of the things he most needs.

Most of us have seen these children who appear to have too much but who really have too little of what they need for healthy growing. There is the little boy who lives down the street or in the next apartment and who seems to have every toy ever invented. He stays up as late as he wants, he can watch any amount and kind of television. He

bullies smaller children, he is "fresh" to adults, he is
constantly boasting about his possessions. But he is also
the little boy whose parents are on the brink of divorce,
absorbed in successful careers; they have little time for
him and he is left in the care of an ever-changing succes-
sion of maids and baby-sitters. Too immature and emotionally unstable to meet their child's real needs, and
guilty over their neglect, his parents have taken the easy
way out of responsible parenthood and have substituted
"things" and unlimited freedom for guidance and love.
Such a child is more to be pitied than censured.

We think of five-year-old Susan as "spoiled" because she
is waited on hand and foot by two doting parents. She is
driven to and from school and she cannot play anywhere
but in her own yard. She runs to her mother with every
little problem and tattles on other children constantly. She
just has to say, "I can't," and whatever it is, her parents
do it for her. Susan's parents were in their late thirties
when she was born. Hoped-for for so long, she is their
wonder and their treasure. No longer as easy-going or as
relaxed as they might have been as younger parents, they
are now overprotective and overanxious. They have not
permitted Susan to test her own strengths, to face up to
the realities of life and learn ways to meet the normal
challenges of childhood. Susan has too much protection,
supervision, and assistance, and because she has no opportunities to test herself, she can have no genuine self-
confidence or pride in herself. She is also a deprived child.

"Things" are not bad in themselves. All children need
an environment that provides the tools of growth, that
stimulates creativity, curiosity, and learning. It is only
when "things" stifle rather than free a child's growth, it is
only when they serve as substitutes for affection, that they
become a hazard.

Freedom cannot spoil a child when it is given wisely
and in relation to a child's readiness to use it. The freedom to experiment, to make choices, is a necessary part
of maturation. The important question is whether it is
provided with careful thought or indiscriminately; whether
it is used or abused.

Love can never spoil a child, for love, in its best sense,
is the feeling for another human being that makes him
feel valued as a person. Genuine parental love permits a

parent to say "NO!" to a child clearly and forcefully when this seems necessary to the best interests of the child; such love is not afraid or apologetic or guilty. It is a kind of love that encourages growth, that reinforces and strengthens a child's own capacities for maturation. Love that is wise, responsible, and freely given makes a child feel that he is wonderful and special and that he deserves the attention, the guidance, the concern, that will help him become a friendly, resourceful, responsible adult.

The spoiled child may appear to live lavishly and freely, but he knows in his innermost being that he would not be given possessions and freedom that are not good for him, that he cannot use well, if he were truly valued as a person. He would gladly relinquish these "things" of which he has too much if someone would only say, "I love you enough to help you grow well."

Possessiveness

In our great eagerness to raise our children to be friendly, kind, and generous, we sometimes overreact to an early possessiveness that really does not persist if we only have the good sense to keep our cool.

The two-year-old screams bloody murder if anyone even touches his rag doll; the three-year-old is ready to bite and scratch and fight to the death anyone who dares to touch his dump truck in the playground; the four-year-old won't let any of the visiting cousins come near her room for fear they will touch one of her eleven dolls.

Unless we carry on, making a great issue out of such events, such possessiveness becomes more moderate with time. If we force children into a generosity that they cannot genuinely feel, we may very well turn them into the hoarders of all time.

At first the young child has a very hard time figuring out where he begins and ends; because it is so terribly important to his feelings of well-being, it seems to make sense to him that teddy bear is really an extension of his own body—he is not sure just where the separation comes, if at all. Young children are also confused about what is animate and inanimate—hence the comment to a hammer and peg, "I'm going to hit you and give you a headache." Some things matter terribly—you can feel amputated if a separation is forced; life without that dirty, familiar, baby pillow just doesn't seem worth living.

A friend of mine was telling her four-year-old the facts of life. She assured him that her uterus was a warm and comfy place where he had been very happy. Danny sighed dreamily and said, "Yes, I remember—I had my special blanket."

When you are not sure of your own self-image—when the edges are still quite blurry—you really cannot afford to let any valued possession leave your side. And when your mother or father insist—when they say that you are mean and selfish for not wanting to share your new wagon with three other kids on the block—then you can only assume that you are quite alone in a friendless world and you had better fight for your own rights, since no one else cares.

At any age, a child has the same right as any adult to love some things too much to share them. When he feels that we will protect his right to these precious belongings, he can relax and let go a little about unimportant things. All children learn by trial and error that if you want to play with someone else's toys, you will have to share yours, or if ten children all want to go on the slide, there is no alternative to bloodshed except taking turns. You need a few years to figure this out—and you need some moral support while you're learning. When Jerry hears his mother say, "Sorry, Fred, Jerry just got that train—it's too new for him to share it—maybe he will later on," he sighs with relief and relaxes; he's got a friend at court. This reassurance is far more likely to make him feel generous than if he had heard instead, "Jerry, if you can't share, I'll take that train away from you."

When company comes—and brings their own preschoolers—parents can suggest that if a child has some very important toys he doesn't want to share, they ought to be put high on the closet shelf; then he won't have to worry, and everybody can play with the less important toys left on display. One mother, in a tiny apartment, with three lively children all sharing a bedroom, gave each of them a box with a lock and a key for their treasures. This friendly gesture, this understanding of their individual rights and needs, led to a far more harmonious sharing of less valued playthings.

Before we push the panic button and come to the conclusion that we are raising a bunch of selfish brats, we might do a little constructive soul-searching. How would we feel about sharing that new antique gold pin or the autographed copy of our favorite book of poems? There is a limit to sharing—and when our children feel assured that we agree, and will respect and honor them in this regard, they can become reassuringly giving. If a neighbor tries to borrow your husband for a fling, chances for borrowing a cup of sugar diminish considerably.

Spanking

My experience has been that if you ask a group of young parents what is the subject that concerns them, very high on the list will be the matter of spanking.

I cannot see any point in discussing whether or not we *ought* to spank our children; it is an irrelevant question. Being human, it seems to me we have to assume that almost every parent who ever lived, hit his kid some time or other. Being human, we get mad and lose our patience, and the swift swat is what happens. Let's accept that as a basic premise of our discussion.

A more legitimate question is, Is spanking a helpful, constructive form of discipline? No, it is not. Unequivocably! It may relieve our anger and clear the air when the atmosphere has gotten pretty tense and wound up, but it does not teach any constructive lessons about human relations, and, after all, that's what discipline is all about: the ways in which we try to teach our children to live in a civilized fashion with themselves and others.

The classic example of the negative teaching involved in spanking was a scene I remember well from the time when my daughter was about three and we were sitting in a park playground. A little boy of about five came over, took a swat at her, and ran off with her pail and shovel. In the midst of trying to comfort my child, wounded in soul as well as in body, I saw Mama descending upon the little boy like a wrathful God, slapping hard and howling, "*This* will teach you to hit someone smaller than you!" It occurred to me that logic was sorely missing in that all-too-familiar scene between parent and child. There seems to be a natural tendency among us parents to teach by negative example. It hardly seems likely that Junior is going to learn very much about not hitting if that is the technique he experiences himself as a parental solution to all problems.

Even when we think we are being most rational about spanking, we are still not teaching any terribly valuable lessons. We say, for example, "I have to give you a spanking in order to make you remember how dangerous it is to run across the road." The lesson there is: "Here I am, a grown-up—a college graduate, even—and the only resource I have at my disposal to teach you the dangers of traffic is physical violence!" What a discouraging picture of human potential!

I believe there is only one appropriate use of spanking—and that is when one is so frightened or so angry or so impatient that one spanks without trying to rationalize or justify it at all; it just happens because you can't help it. You and your child know that it is resorting to the lowest possible level of human interaction and that you don't approve of it, but that sometimes things just get to be too much. If, after such an episode, you are so awash with guilt that you cannot even talk to your child about it, he learns that one should feel very guilty about being human and therefore imperfect. If, out of guilt, you try to find a justification, such as "I had to do that to make you understand," you are still in trouble, because you did *not* do it with premeditation, so you are just plain lying to salve your own conscience. If, on the other hand, you feel a normal and civilized amount of guilt for a fall from

grace and can apologize quite honestly and straightfor-
wardly, both you and your child can pick up the pieces
and move on to some better way of communicating with
each other.

Parents sometimes underestimate the importance of
being able to say "I'm sorry" to a child. It is one of the
best lessons in discipline, for its message is simply this:
"People sometimes lose control. If they are decent, sensible, grown-up people, they try hard to be reasonable, but
sometimes they lose control, because living with kids
can be pretty trying sometimes. But the great thing about
human beings is that they can always strive to improve."
That's an important lesson; it is an example to our children. It suggests that they, too, being human, will falter,
and that it will not necessarily be fatal; they too, will be
able to make amends and continue growing. It is, essen-
tially, a decent and hopeful view of man—that he has his
weaknesses, for which he is sorry, but that he also has his
strengths, and he keeps trying to bring these to higher
levels of development.

The job of being a grown-up parent, is, of course, to try
to increase our sensitivity, our responsibility, so that we
resort to primitive behavior as infrequently as possible—
and so that we certainly don't try to justify brutal or
harshly punitive actions as being worthy of the label
"sound discipline." At the same time it is not necessary to
get out the sackcloth and ashes or to give ourselves thirty
lashes when we spank. Children are great forgivers; they
know when we are scared or when we have reached the
end of our endurance, and they do not see our momentary
loss of control as a terrible threat to their well-being.
Quite the contrary; when you are little and weak and very
much in the grip of impulses you often cannot control, it
is very comforting to discover that those giants of
strength, your parents, have their imperfections, too.

Spanking has no great lessons to teach about wisdom
and self-control, but until some sort of mutant—a new
species of superior men—arrives on this planet, we are
stuck with it.

The gray hairs we parents accumulate prematurely often have to do with our fears that our children will behave in ways that are hazardous to life and limb. It is often difficult to make an accurate distinction between recklessness and a child's natural instinct to be active, to try new things, to develop new skills, to be adventurous and curious. What may look like recklessness can sometimes be inexperience combined with a valid wish to develop a new skill. On the other hand, what may look like healthy courage and a pioneering spirit can sometimes turn out to be recklessness. The distinction is an important one since parents want to protect their children from real danger, but also recognize the importance of permitting children to learn, to increase their skills, through experimentation and direct experience.

There are a number of clues we can use in judging if a child is reckless. An important consideration is whether or not a child has some awareness of what is involved in the thing he wants to do. When a two-year-old runs into the road or a three-year-old blithely walks into the ocean, it is obvious they do not understand the dangers involved. This is a kind of recklessness based on lack of experience—a lack of information about the purpose of traffic lights and the necessity for knowing how to swim before one goes into deep water. Parents are quite right in stopping such behavior and seeing to it that children are protected from reckless acts based on immaturity and lack of readiness.

A second criteria that may be helpful is whether or not a child does have an awareness of what is involved in an experience and is able to proceed with caution. A four-year-old who wants to try to climb to the top of the jungle gym has already had experiences with balancing, climbing, holding on tight, and looking down from high places; he's

22

already been on a slide, he's jumped from the porch steps, he's balanced on a swing. His wish to do something new includes an understanding of the skills he will need. Beyond this awareness, how does he proceed? Does he try to climb halfway up first, or does he try for the top the first time? A child who thinks that the first time he gets on a horse he can gallop, is reckless; if he is willing to walk for the first few lessons, and has the patience and good sense to know he must learn many skills before he can gallop, he is not reckless. If we observe children carefully, we soon see that some children who seem most daring are really just well-coordinated; they know what they can do, and when they say they are ready to try something new, they really are. Recklessness occurs when a child is not able to gauge his own ability or the steps he must take to achieve his goal.

Another way of judging what is reckless behavior has to do with the fact that recklessness is usually motivated by reasons other than just wanting to learn and grow. There is a difference between the child who loves to climb a tree just for the fun of it and the child who climbs on a dare, to gain attention and admiration from his playmates. There is a difference between the youngster who wants to try to swim across the lake to challenge himself and to develop his skills, and the child who tries to do this in order to gain approval from his father who is a great athlete and admires such prowess more than anything else his child might accomplish. When children seem to be struggling for success primarily in order to gain approval, attention, or acceptance that they have not achieved in other ways, rather than for their own enjoyment of the activity, they are more likely to become reckless and take unnecessary chances.

Some children are not merely reckless occasionally, but have repeated accidents of a relatively serious nature. Accident-proneness is usually associated with pretty complicated needs that are not being met in more constructive or positive ways. Here the wish for attention, for comfort, for dealing with inner anxieties by being hurt, are likely to be so complex that special guidance may be necessary in order to help a child find healthier satisfaction of his needs.

Adult supervision and a relatively safe environment can

minimize the hazards, but the only way to grow is to try new things, the only way to overcome inexperience and ineptness is to practice some more. We *do* have to permit our children to take some chances—there is no way of completely avoiding danger at any time in one's life. What we can do to minimize the inevitable bumps and scratches is to protect the very young child from doing what he cannot yet understand, help the more aware child learn caution and patience, and try to help all children to increase their skills for their own inner satisfaction—not to prove themselves to anybody else. To want to explore the world and extend one's own capacities is to be most truly alive; to take chances in order to impress others is recklessness.

Running Away

There is a charming children's story called "The Runaway Bunny" by Margaret Wise Brown.* It begins this way: "Once there was a little bunny who wanted to run away. So he said to his mother, 'I am running away.' 'If you run away,' said his mother, 'I will run after you. For you are my little bunny.'"

Now *there* is a rabbit who knows what she is doing! As regards running away from home, as parents we often don't. Frequently we misinterpret what children are really trying to tell us and ask us when they threaten to leave home.

Most of us can recall the times when as children we felt angry enough at others and sorry enough for ourselves to think of "hitting the road." As parents we accept this as a normal part of growing up unless it becomes chronic and suggests some deeper problem; otherwise we tend to treat it lightly. One of the ways we try to seem nonchalant under such circumstances is to agree with our child that

* New York: Harper & Row Publishers, Inc., 1942.

perhaps he does need a change. One mother reported that when her eight-year-old entered the living room carrying a suitcase, she offered to provide a picnic lunch. But while she was busy wrapping the hard-boiled eggs in waxed paper, her small daughter suddenly burst into tears.

The mother of an adopted boy who had previously lived in many homes and received little love described how much she and her husband had wanted to show their son that they really cared about him. Once, when he ran away, they were afraid to be too severe with him. In their uncertainty, they asked him what they should do. Without a moment's hesitation, he said, "If you love me, you better not let me do that again!" Children want to know that someone will set limits if they can't do it themselves, and yet, in trying to indicate that they do not take the threat of running away too seriously, many parents play along with their children and offer to help them pack—saying, in effect, "We're sorry to see you go, but if you want to leave, I guess there's nothing we can do about it."

I think sometimes we misunderstand the challenge we are being presented with when a child threatens to run away. We know that usually anger—his or ours or both— is involved. "I'll show you," the child is saying. "I'll run away and never come back and then you'll be sorry!" Sometimes a youngster will want to run away as a way of avoiding some problem or challenge which he feels he has failed to meet, or cannot meet. His impulse expresses the hope that he will be missed, that we cannot get along without him no matter what may be wrong at the moment, for deep inside he knows perfectly well that he is helpless. The threat is really an entreaty—he is really asking, "If I get angry or afraid and feel like leaving, will you let me go?" All children want to believe that no unhappy feelings or anger on their part could ever persuade us to let them go. The child wants to feel that even though his own sense of reality is distorted by his feelings, his parents, wiser than he and always loving, will set realistic limits to what he is allowed to do, and that under no circumstances would the adults on whom he is so dependent ever accept his departure as a solution to the problems at hand.

Children are frequently overcome by their own impulses, and at such times they want and need to be able to count on us to help them deal effectively with reality. In many situations children who are permitted to do just as they please become frightened and insecure—and the threat to run away seems to me to be one of those situations in which they are asking for parental controls. What they may really be saying is, "I feel like running away, but we both know I can't take care of myself, so for heaven's sake don't let me do it!"

Looked at in this light, the threat to run away takes on different dimensions. Besides expressing a momentary flare-up of anger, a feeling of being misunderstood, a wish to escape from some frustration or some problem that seems impossible to solve, it also expresses an equally strong wish to be reassured, to feel loved and protected, and to know that momentary feelings and impulses that are totally unrealistic will be stopped, controlled, by protective parents who will see to it that things don't get out of hand.

How then can a parent handle such a situation? He will try to accept and understand the child's feelings, he will acknowledge the child's wish to escape, but—and this is the crucial issue—at the same time he will make it clear that such matters can and will be dealt with *within* the family. Like the mother rabbit, he will say, "If you run away, I will run after you." What a relief it is to the potential vagabond to know that running away is *not* an acceptable solution to the ordinary anxieties and frustrations of family life! In addition to being the truth, it also saves a youngster's pride, for deep down, he is only too aware of his fundamental helplessness—his vulnerability and dependence on caring adults. What he wants to hear is, "Under no circumstances will we let you leave until you are grown-up and can really take care of yourself."

The underlying question, "Would you let me go?" needs to be answered with a firm and absolute "No." That is really what the child wants to hear, for he is a most reluctant traveler!

Showing Off

Few things can exhaust a parent faster than a crazy clown of a kid, showing off for all he's worth. Even the most easygoing parent shudders at the spector of Susy standing on her head on the coffee table or Johnny doing a jig while unsuccessfully juggling something that's wet and leaves permanent stains on the carpet.

Some degree of showing off is an inevitable part of childhood, for in essence, showing off is an amateur's approach to getting attention and recognition while at the same time bravely covering up and compensating for feelings of uncertainty, shyness, and overexcitement.

However normal showing off may be, it can get out of hand and leave both adults and children somewhat unhinged. There are certainly times when adults have to step in and help children gain control of themselves and find more acceptable ways of making their presence felt. Parents can avoid excesses in showing off by an awareness of a child's needs and by some advance planning. For example, a wise parent will know that if doting grandparents, aunts, and uncles are coming for Thanksgiving Dinner and will undoubtedly make a wild fuss over the adorable and beautiful three-year-old sister all day long, nine-year-old Ted is more than likely to let out a war whoop by midafternoon and show off with whatever antics he can dream up to get a little of the spotlight himself. If Ted can be prepared in advance for some of this, if he can be given some very special nine-year-old responsibilities, he may not feel quite so upstaged by his sister's feminine wiles. He might make holiday decorations, or place cards, or crayon some paper plates for serving the potato chips or cookies. He might help with the cooking, or he might prepare a couple of simple magic tricks for after-dinner entertainment. He might be put in charge of

27

serving the canapes or after-dinner mints. Legitimate lime-light, planned in advance, can be more satisfying for both audience and performer.

The child who shows off with other children, who seems "all wound up," overexcited, and silly at a birthday party, may be covering up his embarrassment at not knowing quite how to behave. Maybe he needs some help in think-ing about what he can do, what his friends will enjoy. Seeing to it that children have some opportunity to prac-tice social skills helps them to become more sure of themselves, less overstimulated, more able to participate in social activities without resorting to showing off. Often special talents and hobbies can provide the means by which parents can help a child channel his natural desire for attention and recognition. One family, loaded with dramatic talent among its junior members, permits the children to present a short, original play to company on special occasions. Or a guest may be invited to visit in a child's room for a few minutes to see an exhibit of stamps or butterflies, a beautiful aquarium, or a photography project. Such attention is a legitimate avenue for feelings of importance and achievement, for having one's skills and interests acknowledged and shared with others.

Unfortunately, parents sometimes encourage and rein-force tendencies to show off by urging a child to perform before company when he really doesn't want to. "Say that little poem you learned," they urge, and turning to the guests, they coo nauseatingly, "You *must* hear this, it's so cute!" Or the equally obnoxious question, "What's the point of your taking ballet lessons if you never want to dance when we ask you to?" Maybe the point is to take the lessons for one's own fulfillment. In any event, there is certainly a difference between pushing a child to perform and helping a child who wants to feel "included" to find constructive ways of participating.

The fact that children show off when they are most ambivalent about their feelings is borne out by the showing off that goes on among boys and girls as they approach puberty. Feeling terribly unsure of themselves as they feel the first unmistakable stirrings of interest in the opposite sex, boys will attempt to prove their manliness by wild and raucous deeds of glory, while girls will seek the attention of boys by the giddiest giggling and the most painfully naïve maneuvers. Caught in that moment of greatest ineptness with the most wish for approval and acceptance, their antics are enough to drive the mildest and most well-balanced parent into a state of almost total personality disintegration!

Fortunately, Nature takes care of the problem of showing off; as these young people mature, they become more poised, more practiced in the social arts. Their showing off becomes more subtle and sophisticated; their communications with each other less noisy and a lot more private. Yesterday's somewhat hysterical show-off becomes tomorrow's sophisticated man of the world, and we parents, unreasonable creatures that we are, find ourselves missing the noise and excitement that once gave us Excedrin headaches!

Eating Problems

After bedwetting and nightmares, the topic most dear to a nursery-school parent's heart is the idea that her darling is slowly starving to death. As I look around at the boisterous, active, hardy-looking characters out on the playground at the nursery school, I sometimes have the feeling I'm losing my mind—for what I hear in parent conferences would make me believe that these children should look as though they had just been released from a concentration camp. According to their mothers they eat like birds—not enough to keep a sparrow alive.

Such feeding problems are strictly a phenomenon of affluence. They are unheard of in the cotton fields of Mississippi, in Apalachia, or in Biafra. They exist only among affluent parents who really know better but find themselves responding to that outdated and outmoded notion, passed down from generation to generation, that fat kids are healthy kids. Somewhere, deep down inside us, there is a Jewish or Italian or Eskimo—or any kind—

of grandmother who knew she had solved the survival problem when she could give a substantial pinch to Junior's cheek. Those old patterns die hard, and when children reach the age of three or four and really need quite limited quantities of food for the kind of growth that is then taking place, parents,—mothers especially— tend to lose their marbles.

At one parent conference both mother and father appeared to discuss the fact that daughter Betsy had "not eaten a thing for six months." Oh, she would drink one or two glasses of milk in the course of a day, and she loved bologna and bananas, and she liked to eat a box of Sugar Frosted Flakes at bedtime, and she loved raisins—but meals—never! Betsy was a skinny stringbean all right— she had grown two and a half inches in the first half year at nursery school, and she was also just about the only child in her class who hadn't been out sick once. But her parents' idea of a proper diet consisted of three meals a day, and anything less seemed frighteningly inadequate to them.

Three- to five-year-olds *do* tend to eat less proportionately than older and younger children. If a feeding problem develops, it is usually because parents refuse to adjust to nature's plan.

One of the real hang-ups at this age level is that it seems to parents that preschoolers are old enough to sit down at the table and eat two or three courses before leaving the table. We need to remember that there is really nothing sacred about three meals a day. It is an invention of man, not part of the natural order of things. There is actually nothing the least bit natural about three meals a day when you are three or four. There you are, with that small stomach and that little appetite, and people want you to sit down in front of what seems to you to be a mountain of mashed potatoes, a hamburger the size of a baseball, and several hundred peas—and not only eat them all at once but sit still while accomplishing this feat. It just doesn't make any sense at all when what you really want to do is keep on playing and nibble on something every once in awhile.

What we suggest at the nursery school is that parents assume that three big meals a day is *not* normal or reasonable for nursery-age children. If and when they want to join the family, fine—but portions ought to be miniscule so that children don't get discouraged before they begin. What makes even more sense is to make it possible for the child to eat five or six times a day, as often as possible encouraging him to help in preparing what is eaten. Eating a box of cold cereal while playing with blocks, gulping down some orange juice an hour later after getting thirsty on a bike ride, taking a picnic egg sandwich to eat in the tree house, stashing some nuts and raisins into one's pocket as one goes to dig in the sandbox, having some milk and cookies at a doll's afternoon tea party, and munching on a frankfurter and raw carrots while watching TV in the evening is eating plenty and doing it comfortably when you are too little for the social habits of what is euphemistically called civilized society.

A chief parental concern is that if you don't teach a child the habit of social eating with the family, he'll always be a bum. I recall the shock and dismay of almost every visitor who saw our four-year-old daughter eating in front of the Howdy Doody Show—a TV thriller of her generation. I was assured that she would never learn to be sociable. At seven or eight she discovered the joys of verbal communication, and meals at the table seemed an excellent opportunity to tell us everything we ought to know. Now, some ten or more years later, we still have a hard time getting a word in edgewise.

Preschoolers are very busy trying to figure out how they can begin the long, slow process towards independence and autonomy. If we indicate great anxiety about what and how much they eat, that becomes the battle ground for testing one's powers. This is one confrontation we can avoid by behaving like reasonably intelligent and rational adults. It doesn't mean becoming enslaved—short-order cooks always ready to come up with a gourmet meal. It does mean relaxing unsuitable, rigid rules and responding to a child's natural style of life—letting him eat informally and frequently and keeping in a supply of nourishing "noshes."

When I was that hysterical mother, sure my child would starve, my pediatrician told me, "At seven she'll develop a hollow leg and you'll never be able to fill her up again." She was right. Those children who eat like birds at three turn into vultures at seven or eight, and when they are fourteen or fifteen, attempts to keep the refrigerator full are doomed to failure and you risk impending bankruptcy.

Night Fears

As I'm sure you "civilians" have observed only too happily (human nature having its mean streak!), child experts have a noticeable tendency to make rotten parents! There are many reasons for the instances in which this dangerous over-generalization is true. One of them is that the things you know best when talking to other people about *their* children are forgotten most quickly when dealing with your own.

An example of this was that when our four-year-old said she was afraid of the dark, I forgot everything I would have explained to any other parent about the natural fears of preschoolers and said idiotically, "There's nothing to be afraid of." Our daughter, a perfect example of the human talent for survival, able even at that tender age to surmount the hazards of living with two psychologists, replied, "Maybe *your* dark is all right, but I'm afraid of *my* dark." That was all the reminder I needed, for of course she was quite right. The dark of the three- or four- or five-year-old *is* dangerous to the child, and all the reassurances in the world won't change that reality.

It is no accident at all that preschoolers have fears—of the dark, of dreams, of shadows on the wall, of animals and thunder. These are the natural accompaniments of the kind of growth that is taking place at that dramatic and awe-inspiring time of life. At this age children have discovered language, and it seems to them to have magical powers. You yell "Mama," and that kind lady comes with dry pants or a hug or a bread and butter sandwich. You say a loud "No," and the whole house seems to go up in smoke. You say "I love you" to Grandma, and she'll give you the shirt off her back. You say "I hate you" to cousin Jeffrey, and that same grandmother will read you the riot act. Words, and the thoughts that go with them, seem very powerful indeed. You have the very strong feeling that some bad or naughty things you *think* about, might really happen—and that accounts for some of those preschool fears. If you think "I hate that baby—I wish they'd take him back," something terrible might happen to him and you'd never forgive yourself. If you think "Daddy's a mean man. He makes me go to bed when I don't want to. I wish he'd fall down and break his leg," you live in awful terror that your thoughts, your words, can bring about the deed.

In addition to the magic power of words, preschoolers are going through the first awareness of what it means to be a human being—a creature who is both devil and angel, who can love and hate, be generous and selfish, compassionate and mean, cooperative and competitive. Every day he is reminded of this strange complex wholeness of life—the dark and the light side of human nature. He doesn't understand it and he certainly doesn't like it. Unless he gets a great deal of help from those who are older and wiser, he will get the foolish idea that people can be *either* good or bad and that he must make this decision. Unless he learns that all human beings are both lovely and awful, and that the best he can do is to understand this and try to control what may be dangerous to express *except* in thoughts, he begins to hate that part of himself which is primitive and uncivilized. His fears represent the projection of his anxiety about rage and hostility and aggressiveness outside on other places and things. His dark is full of danger—dangers that are really within himself.

When a child says he is afraid of the dark, we need to accept his fear and help him with it. A night light, a light in the hall and bathroom, staying with him until he falls asleep, may be part of that help. But the more important part is how we help a child see that dark for what it is—not by becoming do-it-yourself analysts, but by letting a child know he has all the same goodnesses and badnesses that every human being on earth has, that thoughts cannot make bad things happen, and that as you grow up, you learn to control impulses and feelings that could hurt other people if you acted them out. You need to learn that you are not a good child or a bad child, only a very little one, and that you need a lot of help from wiser grown-ups who can help you accept your feelings but control your actions. The dark becomes less frightening as each child becomes a friend of his own inner dark—as he accepts the darker side of his own nature and begins the long, slow process of learning to live with it.

The most foolish and useless thing one can say to a child is "There's nothing to be afraid of." If he's afraid, it's real. The reality may be in his own mind, but there's nothing more real than that. I hope I remember this better with my grandchildren!

The War
and Young Children

I couldn't have been more shocked by a statement made by Dr. Bruno Bettelheim, Psychiatric Director of the Orthogenic School in Chicago, in a conversation with a group of young mothers quoted in a woman's magazine some time ago. One of the mothers had brought up the fact that her four-year-old son was asking questions about the war in Vietnam and she didn't know whether or not she should tell him that his parents were opposed to the war. Dr. Bettelheim urged her in no uncertain terms to keep her mouth shut—that young children are unable to understand that some person or nation can be both good and bad—that it is all too confusing. He even went further and suggested that today's hippies—whom he doesn't admire at all, to put it mildly—must have been children who were told about the imperfections of the United States when they were children. Let me quote directly from what he said:

Your child at three or five cannot comprehend that somebody can stink and be great in different situations at different times . . . I don't like the war in Vietnam, but I also know that a man without a country isn't much of a man. That's why I think we should raise our children with a country . . . While there are many different things that make a hippie, one important ingredient is the conviction that whatever this country does is wrong. So if you want to increase your son's chance to be a hippie . . . be sure to tell him that we are wrong in Vietnam. . . . If you're four years old, how can you love your country and oppose this, that and the other? You'll end up with those people who drop out of life . . .

Purely on psychological grounds I would disagree entirely that four-year-olds cannot comprehend the idea that a person or a nation can be both good and bad. As a matter of fact that concept is *exactly* what preschool-age children *are* discovering and beginning to come to terms with. What four-year-old doesn't know that mommies can sometimes be patient and kind and sometimes screaming monsters? What four-year-old isn't discovering the wide range of his *own* feelings—that he can have feelings of tenderness and compassion for his friend Joe, when he cuts his foot, and that he can be ready to murder him a half hour later when he wants his truck back and Joe won't give it to him. Learning about mixed feelings and human fallibility—the broad range of human goodness and badness, wisdom and folly—is the central theme of life for three- to five-year-olds and accounts very largely for bad dreams, animal phobias, fear of thunder, and so on. These fears are the expression of a kind of inner shock at what one is discovering about being human—and the more we, as parents, help a child to accept the full range as normal and necessary, the more a child can come to live in reasonable comfort with the light and the dark side of his own very human nature.

It is perfectly true that a four-year-old can be pretty mixed up and puzzled by any information dealing with complex political issues; for one thing, he very likely wouldn't be terribly interested—the wars and the peace treaties made and broken every day in the sandbox are enough for him to handle at the moment. It would be foolish to make a federal case out of what one is doing or saying about the war, but certainly when a child asks questions, these ought to be answered honestly.

It would seem to me to be quite appropriate and reassuring for a parent to say, "Countries are like people— sometimes they do wonderful things and sometimes they do dumb things or bad things. When people are grown-up, they care very much that their country should try to be the very best it can be, and so, in this country, where we can think for ourselves and say what we think, we are trying to fight for what we think is right." My own feeling would be that parental guidance of this kind is the best way in the world to raise children who will be dreamers and idealists, and if Dr. Bettelheim wants to call them hippies, that's OK with me!

But there is more than psychology at stake here. Let's say, for the sake of argument, that it would be very frightening and confusing to talk about the war in front of young children—what would we do then? Suppose a four-year-old, after overhearing a conversation in nursery school, comes home and says, "Daddy, Jerry's father says we could win the war if we used atom bombs on those bad people," or suppose he asks, "Is this a good war, Daddy?" According to Dr. Bettelheim's point of view you would either have to change the subject or lie.

There are no situations in which something can be sound psychologically if it is not also sound morally and ethically. And those basic value judgments have to be made by each set of parents, alone with their own consciences. Whether one is for the war or against it, one presumably has an opinion, and to pretend that one does not, seems to me to be just about the worst lesson in living one could impose on a child, for it suggests that one can live without principles.

As parents, it seems to me we have a responsibility to do all we can to help our children understand any issue that confronts them. If a child is old enough to be given some kind of an answer, if he is old enough to be aware of a social problem, then he is old enough to need help in finding some acceptable and helpful way of handling his observations.

Of course one must always keep in mind the level of maturity and life experience of a youngster, and when questions are asked, of course we will try to answer simply and without creating undue anxiety. It is very important to know as much as possible about the psychological development of children at different stages, so that when we answer questions on any subject, we will do so in the most helpful and constructive way; there is surely no argument on that score. But the thought that it is *ever* inappropriate or harmful to disclose to one's children the fact that the world and we are imperfect, and that the glorious struggle is to do what we can to make it better, is to rob a growing child of a significant reason for being alive.

Children and Chores

High on the list of any discussion about what bothers parents most about their children's behavior is their attitudes toward chores. "How do you get a nine-year-old to put his pajamas away?" one mother will ask—and twenty others will laugh ruefully and with immediate sympathy and understanding. Another mother will get the same response when she says, "Honestly, I think we ask so little of our kids—and no matter how I nag or threaten or punish, it's a war everytime I ask Peter to straighten up his room or put dirty underwear and towels into the hamper." There is immediate and vociferous agreement that our children are spoiled, lazy, irresponsible, and uncooperative about the simplest chores no matter how intense and forceful our efforts to produce more acceptable behavior may be.

Undoubtedly there is much that is not new about these concerns; parents have always tended to read too much about the future into the present. We find Johnny lying on the grass reading a comic book when he is supposed to be raking up the leaves, and we wonder what will happen when he's in college—will he be goofing off during exam week? We ask Lauri to do the dishes, and the next morning we find that they were done so sloppily and are so greasy that we have to do them all over again, so we conclude too quickly that as a young housewife she will live in a filthy swamp. For whatever comfort it may be, these predictions of adult depravity based on childlike and childish characteristics tend to be highly inaccurate! In the past as in the present, no child worth his salt is likely to have the slightest interest in what seems to him the entirely unnecessary order his parents are so eager to bring into his and their lives! Most children simply cannot fathom what we are so bothered about. Order in their terms usually means having what you need when you need it, and they have no difficulty finding the pair of sneakers they need (behind the bed) or keeping track of their growing rock collection (safely stored on top of the underwear, next to the dead frog, in the dresser). After a busy day of doing *important* things like playing baseball or climbing trees or trading the pet turtle for a Captain Marvel flashlight, what possible difference can it make if one finds one's pajamas on the floor under the transistor radio instead of hanging up in the closet? This battle of differing points of view and priorities is not at all a new phenomenon, and like parents before us, we will survive! There have always been rambunctious, lively, rebellious youngsters who have caused their parents anxious moments of self-doubt and serious misgivings. We take what comfort we may from such old notions (and true!) that "children will be children."

But after all that is said and done, I think we are still more uneasy than parents before us; there is something new and different about our concern. We are really worrying about the larger issue of what work means in the lives of our children. The nature and meaning of work have changed so profoundly in our own lives that we aren't at all sure what we want to teach our children about it. Much of our discomfort about their attitudes toward work reflects our own confusion and uncertainty about the social forces which have so dramatically effected our own attitudes toward it.

Ruminating about all this one night at the dinner table, I asked our teen-age daughter what she thought about work. Her immediate and unhesitating reply was "Work should be fun and interesting." She startled me; would any

generation before hers have thought of work primarily in
relation to fun? In any previous generation the spontaneous response to any question about work would have
been, "Work? Why that's how we stay alive!" Just that
simple and uncomplicated—a matter of survival. We are
facing the serious and challenging question of how to
interpret the meaning of work to our children during a
period of such rapid social change that we are no longer
at all sure ourselves what work really means.

A number of years ago we took our daughter and
several of her friends to visit the restoration of the first
settlement at Plymouth Rock. There was a look of wonder
and shock on their faces when the guide told them that
children as young as three years of age had to begin to
learn to weave and spin; that seven- and eight-year-old
boys worked beside their fathers, plowing the fields, building houses, and making tools; that by the time a pioneer
daughter was twelve she could sew all her own clothes,
make soap and candles, grind corn and bake bread; that in
fishing and whaling towns, boys as young as nine or ten
were apprenticed to sea captains and might have their
own fishing boats before they were twenty. None of this
was for fun or recreation; it was the deadly serious business of learning how to survive in a tough and dangerous
wilderness.

One doesn't have to go back this far in time to see how
life has changed. When most of America was still largely
agricultural less than a century ago, children were an
economic asset, a necessary resource for family survival.
Every member of the family was a needed worker—there
was no other way to get the work done to keep the family
sheltered, clothed, and fed. With the coming of the in-
dustrial revolution and city living, children were still an
economic asset; everybody went to work in the factories
and mines as quickly as possible so that there would be
enough money to buy the necessities of life.

Many of us who are now raising our own children are
old enough to remember when dirty clothing was boiled in
an enormous pot on the stove, when oatmeal had to cook
overnight, and when baby foods had to be strained by
hand every day. In such a world nobody really had to
teach a child lessons about work; he was born into a
world of shared work and he knew, almost before he

could walk, that he was a *needed* worker. This is a world that we may remember only dimly, but it is a world our children never saw at all; and we are faced with a dilemma never dreamed of by our ancestors: how do you get the children to help with the chores when they know darn well we don't *really need* them?

Our notions about work have also changed in relation to the educational expectations we have for our children. Up until the past fifty years, formal academic schooling was not nearly as important as it is today. Most of the survival skills had to do with learning crafts—learning to *do* more than learning to *know*. A child who could learn to make shoes or build boats or milk cows could have a feeling of worth and a hopeful view of his future; he could do something of value. The sixteen-year-old girl who went into the garment factory and learned to run a sewing machine didn't feel like a second-class citizen if she only had an eighth-grade education. In today's labor market we have no room for early "do-ers"; we require all our children, whether or not they are so constituted, to become thinkers and know-ers. If some of our children seem lazy and unmotivated, it may be partly because they were born in the wrong century—for them! If we find it difficult to interest our offspring in making their beds and putting away their toys and clothes, it may be that we are underestimating the kinds of pressures with which they live. It may be true that our children are lucky that we are enlightened enough not to permit them to work as juvenile slaves in mines and factories, but we are kidding ourselves if we think our children are not often enslaved in new ways. How many of our children would prefer to go to work than to battle the New Math or struggle through examinations until they are twenty!

Despite change in our way of life, we know that work— the ability to do a job, to feel the satisfaction in a job well done—is still an essential in human experience. The challenge which confronts parents today is how to give children a new sense of the meaningfulness of work without the element of survival-necessity.

One of the problems is that the jobs we tend to give children to do are terribly dull and inconsequential. They are the jobs we feel sure they can do; we never let them wash the dishes until we are sure they won't break every third one, so they feel no sense of challenge. They also tend to be the chores that *we* despise doing ourselves, so we end up teaching the exact opposite of what we want to teach: instead of demonstrating that work today can be a challenge to oneself, we are teaching that work is an unpleasant duty to others. One mother's attempt to solve this problem was by having every member of the family share the menial tasks equally, and at the same time every child got his chance to take on something more exciting, such as cooking a meal, planning a family picnic, or shopping at the supermarket. "We start when a child reaches his fifth birthday," this mother told me. "And you would be amazed at what a damn fine meal a five-year-old can prepare—if you're crazy about peanut butter and jelly, that is!"

Household chores must still be done, whether or not they are matters of life or death. We could probably save a lot of time and energy if we were to acknowledge how dull and boring we find these tasks—but how much we enjoy the end results. With this orientation, we are better equipped to answer our children when they say "What for?" when we ask them to put away their toys or straighten out the record cabinet in the living room. The answer can be honest and realistic; it is to give us all a comfortable, attractive place in which to do the things we enjoy doing. However, we need to be clearer in our own minds about what necessity really means in our homes. How often do we demand a kind of perfection in orderliness that really has little or nothing to do with this goal of comfort? Aren't there many tasks that could be eliminated or modified?

One way to find sensible answers to this question is to think in terms of what will give a child the satisfying feeling that he is really needed. The world will not come to an end if Junior doesn't take out the garbage or mow the lawn or wash the car. Getting him to do these jobs doesn't make him feel needed, so while we may still see good reasons to demand his cooperation in some such tasks, we might think about dividing them up more equally among all the family members. We might, on occasion, sit down with our children and talk to them about what *they* think is needed. Maybe they think the dog needs a longer run in the back yard, or they need a more spacious shed for outdoor toys; maybe they have some practical ideas for creating more shelf space in the playroom or building a desk-top that can be folded up against the wall to save space in their bedroom. We might all discuss together how these important-to-them projects can be carried out, for they will learn far more about the real meaning of work by what makes sense to them than by simply carrying out our orders for things *we* think are important.

We need to be careful that we don't interfere too much in those jobs that our children do, but imperfectly. Too often we fill in when a child does something that doesn't live up to our higher standards, so he can't feel any genuine sense of accomplishment. A four-year-old dusts the dining room table, shows it to us with pride, and while we are saying "That's lovely, darling," we are absentmindedly finishing the job to our satisfaction. Part of learning to enjoy work is to be permitted to execute and complete it to *our* satisfaction, not someone else's. When seven-year-old Debbie makes you an apron with one fat tie and one skinny tie, that's the way it ought to stay if we want her to go on to other pleasures in sewing-all-by-yourself.

Some drudgery falls into the most glamorous of lives—this is a fact about household chores that must be accepted and tolerated. Our children need to understand that you can't love what you are doing all of the time. Some things just have to be done in order to reach a goal. For a three-year-old this may mean, "If we clean up your toys together, we will have time for a story." For a five-year-old it may mean, "If you put your bicycle in the garage every night, it won't get rusty." For a nine-year-old it may mean, "If you help me with my chores—save me some time by watering the lawn—I'll be able to drive you down to the high school football game on Saturday."

What we have to communicate to our children is that cooperation is good human relations and that this is just as important as it ever was. We need to be clear in our own minds that there is no inborn instinct that will drive a child to shoulder responsibilities that annoy or bore him. It wasn't strength of character that drove Greatgrandpa to the woodpile after school every day—it was the sure knowledge that there would be cold winter nights if he didn't do his job. We can't pretend with our children that what we ask of them is nearly so vital, but we can make it clear that sharing what has to be done, however unexciting the jobs may be, is an expression of love and a sure road to self-respect. Despite affluence and automation, the family is still a cooperative enterprise. One mother put it succinctly when she said, "When I ask Jeff to do something that he thinks is just another of my compulsive stupidities, before he even asks why, I say, 'For love, that's all, just for love!' "

One of the complications we face in getting chores done, is that a great many of us *could* afford to hire someone to do the jobs we ask our children to do. When I expressed horror that a friend was having trouble finding a new gardener—the lawn hadn't been mowed for three weeks—she said, "You're right. We do have three able-bodied sons, and it's disgusting—but they know darn well I can afford to hire someone." We have to make it clear that money has nothing to do with self-respect and that the lack of an economic motive does not make work obsolete. A father told me recently how distressed he was by a conversation he had had with his sixteen-year-old, who wanted to spend the summer vacation "just loafing around." This father had suggested that Ken at least try to find a part-time job. He agreed that Ken had worked hard in school all year, but did not agree that doing nothing for two months made any sense. Ken argued that it was silly to get a job—he didn't need the money. He said, "It's not costing you anything. You don't even have to give me an allowance if you don't want to—I have enough saved up." His father replied, "It isn't a question of money, *it's what you are doing with your life that matters.*" Even much younger children can begin to discover that meaningful work has to do with personal fulfillment, not necessarily with monetary considerations. But if work has more to do, today, with personal development, this implies that we must give children a sense that they are working for their own goals, not for ours. Work used to be for one's parents; many of us grew up in an era when we can remember very well that we thought a great deal more about pleasing our parents than ourselves. I think we want our children to work hard for what *they* will gain from their own accomplishments, and we have to make some clear distinctions about this to our children. One father told me that when his nine-year-old son was doing sloppy homework assignments, he told him, "Jerry, you have to make your own decision about this; if you write your work sloppily, it won't matter whether you have the right answers or not— your teachers are going to be angry at your laziness and you will get lower marks. It doesn't seem important to you right now, but as time goes on, you are going to want to get credit for what you can really do, and the only way that will come about is if you care more how you present your work. If you decide you don't care, I'm not going to lose my job, and Mom won't be kicked out of the PTA— the only one who will suffer will be you." Having made that crystal-clear, we have the even harder task of sticking to our guns; we simply must let our children follow through on such decision-making issues no matter how long it takes. We have to *mean* it when we say, "It's what you do with *your* life, not mine."

Autonomy and self-direction can also be encouraged when we look for more opportunities for children to satisfy themselves through work. We are going to have to become more flexible about such things as how a child takes care of his room—or doesn't. If it's really his room and he loves his personal garbage dump, is it really so terrible if he only cleans it up once or twice a month, so that the room can be vacuumed and properly aired? Does he learn about the significance of work when we nag him every day to do a job *he* thinks is entirely unnecessary? If we leave him alone, or work out a compromise, we need not feel we are destroying his character or moral fiber, so long as there are other work opportunities that *do* help him to see what work is really all about. This means reversing an old pattern in which most of us are caught. We should nag less about chores, but demand more and expect more of our children when it comes to their working for their own goals. By that I mean, for example, our too-quick purchase of anything our children want us to buy for them.

If I were starting out all over again as a young mother, I know that there is one area of child raising in which I would change my ways drastically. I think about it (painfully!) everytime I see the expensive guitar we bought, lying on the floor, its strings sprung; or the typewriter, all wound up in its old ribbon, used maybe for a month; or the sewing machine gathering dust on the closet floor, used to make one dress and then never used again. I yelled too much about cleaning up, and I was too permissive and easygoing about satisfying every childish whim. If we had insisted that there had to be some real effort on her part to acquire special things, I think they would have meant more to her—but even more important, the process of acquisition itself would have been such an important experience in learning what work can mean that I don't think I would have felt so angry and frustrated when they too might have been set aside or discarded.

We need to help our children see that we do not think of work in a narrow way, as only being related to how one earns one's livelihood. We can each find those work activities that stretch our talents and that serve others, that fire the imagination and that make us feel needed. The essential quality in this view of work is that it can take many forms, vocational and avocational, but that it is important to find work that one needs for self-respect and personal fulfillment.

With less time needed to devote to household chores, there will be time for useful work in the communities in which we live and creative work on our own; there is honorable and pleasurable work for all of us to do that makes us feel good, that gives us a sense of well-being and pride in our accomplishments. Children can begin to feel needed for the contributions they can make. In one family, a two-dollar contribution is made to UNICEF everytime a child mows the lawn. In another, a teen-ager is relieved of all dishwashing because he gives two afternoons a week to teaching children to read in a special volunteer teaching program in a deprived neighborhood. In still another household, all major household cleaning is done by the whole family on Saturday mornings so that Mother and her two youngsters can have the free time during the week to take ceramics and dancing classes.

There has never been a time when young people had more scope, more variety of opportunities to find the work that will be meaningful and fulfilling. Our children can realistically expect to find work that they will enjoy doing—there is nothing sinful or immoral in that! Sometimes it will be the work they do to earn a living, sometimes it will be the work they do that has nothing to do with earning a living; the important thing will be knowing that to be most truly and joyously alive one must work.

To conclude, I think my daughter was right—in today's world it is reasonable to assume that most of one's work *can* be fun and interesting! I think we ought to accept our children's orientation toward work in these terms—but we must help them to see this in its broadest meaning; fun is when you feel challenged to do your best, when somebody needs you, and when you are proud of what you are doing.

On Being Fair

One of the most difficult challenges in being a parent is that children frequently do not say what they really mean. We find ourselves responding to their *words,* rather than to the background music. And then, when we begin to realize that our responses have been meaningless or futile, we despair of being good enough detectives to figure out what is really going on.

A good case in point is what happens when our children tell us that we are not being fair: Johnny got a bigger piece of cake than Suzy, an older child complains that a younger one stays up just as late, Karen is mad because Jeff was allowed to buy a comic book on a shopping trip, but no one brought her one. Because it is of course impossible to love any two human beings in exactly the same way, we become frightened by the challenge "You're not being fair." We wonder if we *are* showing partiality— we try to mend our ways. It seems to me that we would be more sure of our ground if we could figure out what that indictment of unfairness really means. Let's take a closer look at some real-life situations:

A mother recently reported that she had solved the bedtime problem at her house. Her three-year-old felt she was being treated unfairly when she had to go to bed before her two older brothers, so mother had talked the boys into pretending they were going to sleep at the same time. Once she was asleep, they were allowed to get up and play a little longer. A father said that he was on his way home from work one night and suddenly had an impulse to get his daughter a gift. She had been quite sick and had behaved very well, and he wanted to let her know he felt proud of her. He started to buy her a toy, then began to wonder if the two younger children would be jealous and think he was unfair, so he bought presents for them, too. When he walked into his daughter's room and gave her the gift, her face lighted up—she got the message—and then, when her father went on to give presents to the other children, her pleasure ended as quickly. He knew that something had gone wrong in his wish not to show favoritism.

Children encourage our confusion about what is fair. They sense very quickly that we are uncertain, sensitive, inclined to be on the defensive. How ought we to respond? It seems to me very probable that the taunt "You're being unfair" is really a challenge—a question: "Am I special? Do you see me as a separate person?" This is more important to all human beings than absolute equality. The little girl mentioned earlier isn't going to be satisfied by her mother's solution to the problem of bedtime for very long, and neither are her brothers. The present brought to the sick child had no special meaning because all three children got something at that moment. How do children really interpret these well-meaning but misguided attempts at equality? Usually as an indication that they are not viewed as separate, distinct human beings. Mother isn't *really* looking at Jane when she makes these complicated sleeping arrangements—if she were, she would say, "I don't care about what anybody else does—*you* are three years old and *you* need more sleep!"

It is actually enormously reassuring to a child when a parent agrees with his complaint of unfairness completely, and says, "Yes, you are absolutely right—I don't treat you and Jack the same way, and I don't give you the same things, because you are two completely different people, and what may be important and good for one may not be for the other." If children find us constantly trying to be fair in some unrealistic way, they are likely to continue to complain of unfairness, even if we eventually get a gram scale and measure everything out carefully! They will continue this complaint because the answer has been unsatisfactory. Frantic attempts at equalizing tell a child that his parents don't see him as a separate person—and that they probably *do* have a favorite, or why would they go to such lengths to disprove it?

The sick little girl needed a special relationship with her father at a special moment in her life—a one hundred-percent relationship of approval and encouragement. The others would have their day in the sun when they needed something special at some other time. Each child wants to feel that at some moments in his life one or both parents are focused on his particular needs, and if we are always giving one quarter or one half of ourselves, no one is ever satisfied. In the long run it is far more comforting to know you have been seen as an individual and that you have not been lumped together with others who have their own differences.

Unfairness goes with individuality. What may be right for one youngster may be wrong for another. Intense caring, individual concern, are far more meaningful than equality. What is *really* fair is when children feel they are being seen separately—when they observe that our sense of justice is based on individual needs and not on comparisons. The outraged cry "You're being unfair!" is a trap. Let's not fall into it. There will be far less weighing of justice in our households when we respond "You're darned right!"

Death
and Young Children

I was standing in line at a neighborhood bank, behind a young mother and her four-year-old son. It was a long line and he was impatient and jumpy. Suddenly a lovely little old lady appeared, carrying two heavy shopping bags, and the little boy almost jumped out of his skin with joy as he pounced on Grandma. Her enthusiasm matched his, and she offered to take him home for lunch where he could wait for his mother. In his glee, he jumped up and down and knocked one of the bags out of his grandmother's hand, and as his mother began to scold him for being too wild, the little old lady suddenly crumpled to the floor of the bank—and died. Of course none of us knew that immediately. The lines of people moved back, someone brought a pillow for her head, somebody else went to call the police, a bank teller ran up the block to see if a doctor was in his office.

I stood and watched this moving drama of life and death for some time. A doctor finally appeared and told the young woman her mother was dead. The daughter explained, "She's had a heart condition for seven years, and we've begged her not to go shopping and carry those heavy bags, but she wouldn't give in." It was clear that Grandma was in her late seventies, that she had lived her life the way she wanted to, refusing to be an invalid, and that she had died with style—still living independently, still much loved, still young in spirit. Her death seemed to me, as an adult, quite comprehensible, inevitable.

Shaken, and deeply moved, it was not until I began to walk out of the bank that I thought about the little boy. Then I remembered his look of unbelieving shock—and I remembered with piercing anguish that he had sat on the floor next to his grandmother, patting her arm and saying "I didn't mean to hurt you." I wanted to run back and tell his mother to be sure and explain that he hadn't killed his grandma with his loving exuberance—that she was a sick old lady and that if she'd had the choice, this was un- doubtedly the way she would have preferred to die—in loving encounter with her grandchild. But we are all terrible strangers in the city, and I didn't have the courage to interfere. I have been haunted by my cowardice ever since, and maybe if I talk to all mothers and fathers, some other little boy can be told something he needs to hear.

All of us ignored the little boy until his grandmother was taken away, and he and his mother began to leave the bank, she weeping and certainly too distracted to think about her son, he wide-eyed with terror. A woman leaned toward the young mother, patted her on the shoulder as she walked by, and said, "At least he's too young to understand."

That is really the heart of the matter. Children are really *never* too young after the age of two or three to understand *something* about death. And what they usually "understand" is a complete misinterpretation of the true events. Young children tend to make self-references about almost every experience when they are little. Jean Piaget, the Swiss educator and psychologist, reported from his observations of children that until the age of nine or ten, the way children think, naturally involves them in every dramatic experience. If parents divorce, the child thinks, "It's my fault. If I wasn't so naughty, they would still love each other." If a grandparent dies, the child's irrational fantasy is, "I guess I killed Grandpa because I made noise in the hall when he was sick." If Daddy has to go away on a business trip, Junior thinks, "I'm not lovable enough to keep him here," while frequently, adopted youngsters, no matter what they have been told to the contrary, believe there must have been something wrong with them or their natural parents could not have given them up.

The young child's experience is so limited that he simply doesn't have the perspective or understanding to recognize causes outside of himself. The little boy in the bank was too young to understand old age and heart disease. To him, Grandma was real and strong and invulnerable. But *he* had been jumpy and restless and his mother was angry at him. And then, naughtiness of all naughtinesses, he had jumped on Grandma. If someone doesn't tell him about death, if everyone thinks he's "too young to understand," if he is pushed aside and not allowed to share the normal and needed grief that the grown-ups will allow themselves for comfort, he may very well close off all his memories of Grandma and grow up remembering nothing of this event, but with a lingering feeling that to love anyone too much and to show it too obstreperously is maybe to kill—to be a dangerous, a bad person.

Whenever and wherever young children experience death, they need our help in interpreting its meaning, in clarifying the fact that they are not responsible. And then they have every right to share in our grief—to cry, to feel deeply sad, to need comforting. When we say we want to protect our children from pain, we really leave them alone with wild fantasies, unshed tears, and great loneliness. We don't mean to, but that's what protection often seems to mean. Children and adults can only surmount grief when they understand the meaning of death and when they share their anguish and seek comfort and strength from each other.

The Adopted Child

I was very happy to hear recently that a child guidance clinic in Philadelphia is now advising parents to be more careful about telling a child he is adopted, and is suggesting that to the degree that it is possible, children not be told they are adopted until they are seven or eight years old.

When adoption first became widespread and a topic openly talked about, perhaps twenty-five or so years ago, social workers, psychiatrists, and psychologists almost universally advised parents to talk to their child about being adopted as early as possible—certainly by three or four. The idea was that if a parent could be very relaxed about it, and if the word "adopted" was introduced into the child's vocabulary very casually, the child would feel that there was nothing wrong or bad about being adopted. This became the era of "The Chosen Baby" approach, with great emphasis on that happy moment of union between parents and child.

Adoptive parents were made to feel that if a child had problems about his adoption, it was because the subject had not been presented comfortably enough or because the difficulties simply reflected problems in the present family relationships. As mental health clinics spread throughout the country, it began to appear that a disproportionate number of children who were being seen were adopted, and because this was the prevailing mood of the times, parents were blamed; it wasn't at all the fact of adoption that could be troubling the child, but only the parents' unresolved problems about being adoptive parents.

Some of us began to have some misgivings about this. It began to dawn on us that with all the emphasis on being a chosen child, quite a hunk of the child's history was being too easily overlooked. Before that moment of being chosen, there *had* been a parental rejection, like it or not. And from a young child's point of view, with his limited experience, there was no possible way in which he could imagine legitimate circumstances that could explain giving a child away. Nothing in his own life experience could make this comprehensible. Nobody *he* knew would ever do such a thing. Until children are well into puberty, the realistic possibilities just don't exist; he cannot imagine the birth of an illegitimate child to two high school sophomores; he cannot imagine a mother of eight who simply cannot afford to take care of another child.

In addition to this basic lack of information, young children have a natural tendency toward self-reference—for assuming that whatever happens is their fault. Typical of this is the adopted five-year-old who has been told over and over again how adorable he was as a baby, who has seen pictures of himself, who has been doted on by grandparents, who suddenly says, "What was wrong with me that they gave me away?"

We have greatly underestimated the fantasy life of the young child—his capacity for making up irrational explanations for things he is too young to understand. Adoption is not all sunshine and flowers; we have oversentimentalized it, thereby screening out our pain as well as the child's in an understandable conspiracy to ignore the unpleasant part of the story.

A young woman once commented to her therapist, "For four weeks I didn't even have a name." That is a painful, deeply human feeling of deprivation. Adoption, whether we like it or not, involves a parental rejection, and this is a fact of life for the adopted child. To some degree at least, there is a sense of lost beginnings, of uncertain identity. Handled with the greatest compassion and understanding, there will still be some scar tissue. Parents need help in facing that fact, so that they in turn can be more helpful to their children.

I have come to the conclusion that while all children must be told—it would be impossible to live with such an enormous subterfuge—it may be better to postpone most discussion of it until a child is over the period of the most irrational fantasying—from about three to six—and has some feeling about himself, some sense of who he is as a person, and can therefore deal with the issue more realistically. Even more important than the question of when to tell, is the larger issue of giving up the myth that "Life Can Be Beautiful." Adoption is a wonderful solution to a serious problem and it can bring great happiness to all involved—but it also has dimensions of pain that must be accepted. That is the nature of life itself, and the adoptive family needs to be de-romanticized and re-humanized.

SECTION
II

Growing Pains
or Neurotic Strains

One of the most difficult questions every parent faces sooner or later is whether or not a particular kind of behavior on the part of a child is simply the sort of thing one can check off philosophically and unconcernedly as normal growing pains, or whether it is a symptom of some neurotic strain that bears watching and perhaps doing something about. How can you tell, these days, when a child is going through a normal phase and when he's in trouble? Pick up any book on child raising and you will discover that all sorts of interesting aberations are considered normal, some of the time. Shyness, fears, bad dreams, lying, temper tantrums, nail-biting, thumb-sucking—you name it—these days they are all listed under normal behavior. And yet, what perplexes and confounds us is that under some circumstances these very same things are viewed as symptoms of distress.

The more we study and learn about children the more we recognize that no one kind of behavior, by itself, need be considered a sign of serious difficulty, but the same behavior, in some situations, may be a sign of disturbance. How can we make the important distinction between a normal phase and a danger signal?

First of all, certain kinds of behavior are more appropriate at certain ages. By learning as much as we can about the broad range of normal growth and development, we can estimate the appropriateness of the behavior. Fear of the dark may be perfectly normal at four but

Eda LeShan

questionable in a ten-year-old; telling wild tales is one thing in kindergarten and something quite different in junior high school; excessive shyness with strangers is different in a three-year-old than in a twelve-year-old. Some understanding of general growth patterns can help us observe children more sensitively and gain in perspective about the meaning of their behavior.

Another criteria for evaluating behavior lies in the importance of "special events" in a child's life. Five-year-old Johnny is wetting his bed; he hasn't done this for a long time, and his mother wonders. Does this mean anything? Her practical husband reminds her that they have just moved from another city and Johnny has his own childlike ways of showing the normal tension of adjusting to a strange room in a strange house on a strange street. Eight-year-old Barbara has suddenly begun to have trouble with her school work, after a very good start—what could it mean? Barbara happens to have become a sister for the first time two months before, and having been an "only" for such a long time makes it a little tougher to see a baby taking center-stage. When a child who has seemed to be happy and productive shows signs of disturbance, we have to ask ourselves has there been any realistic change that may cause a temporary setback. The kind of tension or anxiety that is related to some specific event isn't likely to persist too long, especially if no one gets too upset about it. In such situations, we need to watch and listen—give children a chance to bounce back, having faith in their recuperative powers and remembering that behavior rather than language communication is a child's way of handling a difficult growth experience.

A third criteria has to do with the difference between an isolated symptom and a pattern of behavior. When Fred gets excited, he stutters a little—his ideas seem to get ahead of his tongue—but he's having a fine time in school, has lots of friends, and seems quite relaxed and comfortable with himself most of the time. Bill stutters too—but he's also been more and more moody and unhappy. For a long time he's seemed to have trouble making friends, his teacher says he can't concentrate on his schoolwork at all, and his parents have noticed that he seems to be becoming more and more fearful of new situations. They feel they can't reach him—whenever they try to talk to him, he becomes sullen or defiant and the stutter becomes much more pronounced.

The difference between Fred and Bill is a crucial one. Fred's satisfactions in life continue—Bill is in a bind. When symptoms seem to increase in number, become fixed, and lead to a kind of general interference with growth and self-fulfillment, it may well be time for some concern.

If I had to pick one kind of feeling that most frequently reflects serious emotional difficulties, it would be the observation that a child doesn't seem to like himself—when we get a persistent feeling that he is unhappy about being the person he is. One can weather almost any of the storms of growing and living if one has a good feeling about oneself—a feeling of being glad to be oneself, a feeling that one is worthy of being loved by others. It is a sense that one can accept the challenges of life and that one brings something special and good into the world just by being alive and oneself. The absence of this zest for living, this basic love of oneself, is perhaps the clearest indication that a child needs help. Of course no one maintains this sense of well-being all the time; here again it is a question of quality and quantity—of steady and consistent feelings of unworthiness.

It's a struggle to grow up—and we need to keep our heads. All of our children must and will experience troubled, turbulent times; that's in the very nature of being human and alive. But we need to be open to the possibility that there may also be times when we find ourselves unable to help a child take the next hurdle, untangle a snag in growing up. This is no sign of failure on our part, nor does it mean that we abdicate from parenthood and let an expert take over. All it means is that life is more challenging and difficult and complex for some human beings than for others, and that the perspective and broader experience of a trained counselor may give us just the lift we all need at a particular moment. It is the strong who seek to be stronger, not the weak and fainthearted. We all bear wounds, being human—and those who seek to be healed are the bravest.

Getting the right kind of help is another matter. When a parent chooses a pediatrician, a dentist, a school or a baby-sitter for his child, he feels confident about using his

own judgment. He may listen to the recommendations of
others, he may look into the background training of those
he is considering—but in the final analysis, his choice will
depend on his personal likes and dislikes. If the pediatrician says "Bring Suzie to the office" when she's running a
fever of 104°—good-bye doctor! If Bobby, usually
robust and outgoing, seems pale and wan on the first
visitor's day at camp, and the performance put on for the
parents seems to rival the Olympics in competitiveness,
Bobby's trunk is packed—good-bye camp. We feel we
have the right and the obligation as parents to make
reasoned, thoughtful, *personal* judgments on such matters.

Too often this is not the case in choosing a therapist.
We have been brainwashed! It is becoming less true as
time goes by, but we still carry the residue of the earlier
attitudes in psychiatry that while the patient operated
entirely on the basis of unconscious and pathological
causes, the therapist always knew what he was doing! As a
result of this double standard, if you didn't like your
therapist, it wasn't anything *he* was doing, but only that
you were unconsciously resisting his ministrations. There
are too many people who have spent two—five—even ten
years in therapy, who have most of the time felt that they
were not making any real progress, who actively disliked
the therapist—but who have continued because, after all,
this was just another clear indication of how sick *they* were!

A mother wrote me recently that she had taken her
six-year-old to a psychiatrist because he seemed too preoc-
cupied with death and dying. She knew this was not an
abnormal concern, and in most other ways her youngster
seemed to have a good life—but she felt it was a little
obsessive, and she wanted to get some help in understanding the possible causes so that she and her husband could
help their child handle these real anxieties. After seeing the
child twice, the psychiatrist told the parents the following:
their son was seriously disturbed; the therapy would take
two years; and during that time they should not consider
moving, under any circumstances, because this would
undo the whole process. Also, during the treatment period
the therapist would have no direct contact with the parents at all—they would consult with a psychiatric social
worker whom he would recommend and all communications would have to be handled through her.

The father, a journalist, could not possibly guarantee that he would not have to move for two years. The mother asked me, "Am I very neurotic to feel that I have a right to some direct conversation with the doctor, that I don't want to have to always go through a middleman?" Even as she asked the question, it was obvious that she did so reluctantly and somewhat shamefacedly, assuming that the doctor *must* be right.

All wisdom and sensitivity does *not* reside on the other side of the desk. As in any profession, there are wise men and fools, rigid, inflexible mechanics and men of enormous compassion and great creative artistry. We must be critical and discerning, especially where children, who cannot defend themselves, are involved. Shopping around is perfectly legitimate. We must find that special human being. Assuming of course, that we seek an individual who is highly trained and has all the necessary credentials, we still must choose for ourselves. What kind of a person is he? What is his overall philosophy of life—and is it in harmony with your own? What are his interests? Is this someone you would enjoy meeting and knowing under any circumstances? Do you have similar goals and ideals? Is it stimulating and rewarding to listen to him? Does he make sense to you about the important and profound issues of life? And most important of all, is he willing to talk about these matters with direct candor or is he secretive and evasive? Does he make you feel like a worthwhile person, someone with inner strength, with courage enough and creativity enough to change?

There are no crystal balls in a genuine exploration of human needs. No one can guarantee results or give you a time schedule. An honest answer of "I don't really know— we'll have to explore this together" suggests a necessary humility and is not an evasion. Natural warmth, spontaneity, and humor are ingredients that are likely to help you to feel that this is a person who can help you come to know yourself better—and like the self you discover.

Beware especially of the orthodox *anything*! If a therapist implies that his breed has all the answers, run, do not walk, to the nearest exit. Men of great wisdom and artistry have contributed to our small treasure of knowledge about human beings, and no school of thought has all the gems. I fell instantly in love with the lady analyst who said, "How can I tell you what school of psychiatry I belong to, until I see the *child*?" A close second was the psychologist who said, "I was trained as a Freudian, and if I learned anything from the Master, it was to learn from every great teacher I could find."

One of the most serious challenges to modern psychotherapy has been the focus on pathology, so that one loses sight of the strengths which people also have, in abundance—especially children. Even though there is a problem, choose someone who is just as concerned with tenderly nurturing what is *right* with a child—his own unique qualities and strengths—as he is with relieving discomfort or anguish. When something is going wrong, it usually means that the very best in a human being is blocked and wants to be free. If we only look at the agony, we can never achieve the ecstacy of personal fulfillment. It is important to choose a therapist who is not interested in seeing to it that your child conforms to some vague social norm, but wants to help him be most truly and deeply himself, for that is the greatest health of all.

Particularly in the case of young children, it seems to me that the parent has not only the right but the responsibility for full partnership with the therapist. It can be made quite clear to the child that he can have some special, private secrets, not for parental ears, but at the same time, Mommy, Daddy, and the doctor are working together as a team and must talk to each other from time to time. It is not an alignment of friends vs. enemies, but three loving, concerned adults, all trying to help.

In twenty five years of working with parents and children I have *never* met a parent who wasn't trying his damndest to do the right thing. No matter how dumb or depraved his behavior might seem, *there was no malice in it*. The helpful therapist assumes that parents have the capacity to change, to become more effective in their struggle to express their love and concern. This does not imply benign approval. I want an expert who trusts me enough to tell me what I am doing that isn't helpful—who challenges me, believes in me, says, in effect, "I respect you enough to tell it to you like it is." This also gives me the option to disagree—and I want to know that my opinions are also valued and respected.

Successful child counseling or therapy is a partnership,

a mutual exploration and search for more helpful and constructive answers. There are no final solutions—only better ways to meet the inevitable frustrations that are part of living: a quest to meet these struggles through being deeply and truly alive and oneself. I have never heard it described any better than by the child who said to his therapist, "I spill my heart out to you, which wasn't in such hot condition, and my heart comes back to me OK."

Sibling Rivalry
Is Here To Stay

During the past half-century of intense focus on childhood, one of the more frequent topics of discussion has been sibling rivalry. Psychologists have been observing and recording the jealousies of brothers and sisters with a jaundiced eye and psychiatrists have been doing their best to heal the inevitable wounds of warfare. Parents have made brave if foolhardy efforts to pretend to their firstborn that the new arrival is a very inferior product and hardly worth noticing at all. Patience, understanding, the artistic referee-ing, while occasionally bringing about a temporary truce, rarely produce a bonafide and permanent cessation of hostilities. Perhaps it is time to face a simple fact; like death and taxes, sibling rivalry is here to stay!

And why not? Isn't it a reality of the human condition that each of us struggles to be special? Do we really need to look at brothers and sisters to discover the quite human characteristics they often display—rivalry and competition and a wish to have infinite love? Is there anything so remarkable or special about the fact that human beings want to be recognized, appreciated, and enjoyed *all by themselves?*

One mother, puzzled by the fact that her older child remained jealous of the new baby, consulted a psychiatrist. She assured him that she had been very understanding and loving. She had explained to her daughter that having one baby had made her so full of love that now her love was overflowing and she had some left over to give to the second child. Shouldn't such an explanation provide adequate reassurance? "Well, let's follow this to its natural conclusion," the psychiatrist suggested. "On the basis of your theory there would be no reason for you to be alarmed or angry if your husband were to come home some evening and say, 'You know, darling, being married to you has been so wonderful that it has made my love expand and grow and now I feel I have enough love left over to take a concubine.'" She got the point.

Even in the relationship of marriage, where both partners have chosen each other after falling in love, where each person fulfills deep and important needs in the relationship, there are inevitable periods of anger and conflict. How much more natural this must be between children who did *not* choose each other, who did *not* start out having any logical reason for loving each other, and who do *not* see how any such relationship can be of any use or purpose. A common characteristic of childhood is to want what you want when you want it. The presence of siblings is a sure guarantee that there is less chance than ever of getting things to run that way. It takes a lot of living for brothers and sisters to discover the very genuine assets available to them; often it takes growing up.

A number of years ago a psychiatrist who had been stationed in Okinawa during the Second World War returned home with a message; he had found a place and a people where rivalry and jealousy between siblings did not exist. He spoke to many parents and child experts, reporting on the child-raising practices that seemed related to these results and exhorting his audiences to go out and do likewise. At one such meeting a colleague arose to discuss his presentation. "Your observations are most interesting, Doctor," she said. "The only problem is that if we try to raise our children as they do in Okinawa, how will our children pass their competitive college boards or ride on the subway during the rush hour?"

Sibling rivalry, viewed in the context of culture, may not be such a bad thing, after all. We live in a society that demands intensity and challenge in human relations, that involves active participation and competition. But it's far more involved than that; the same society that sometimes appears to encourage a "dog-eat-dog" approach is also the society of enduring and pervasive compassion, tenderness, and nurturance. It is, in other words, as ambivalent as sibling relations. The relationship of brothers represents a microcosm of the relations of all men.

It is not especially fruitful for parents to spend much time reflecting on whether sibling rivalry is instinctive and inborn or represents social and cultural pressures. In our society most families have ample opportunity to discover that wherever it came from, it exists as a reality of life. Many parents share the feeling that there has been too much time and energy spent on analyzing, describing, and trying to eliminate sibling rivalry. Perhaps it is time to grin and bear it!

That doesn't necessarily mean hiding one's head in the sand and hoping it will go away if ignored, or hopelessly enduring it without trying to modify or alleviate it at least enough to make it bearable! If you have to live with something that tends to produce loud noises and general unrest and upheaval, it makes good sense to do what you can to tone it down to a reasonable endurance level. One psychiatrist took the position that a reasonable goal that parents might set for themselves is "The avoidance of bloodshed!"

There are a number of techniques and attitudes that *can* serve to *minimize* the chaos and that may represent a survival kit for parents. A first rule that one might follow is that sibling rivalry must be accepted without fear or embarrassment. There is really no reason why one's firstborn should be delighted at the obvious usurpation of his power. What healthy red-blooded American child in his right mind wants to give up being the center of the universe? If siblings, who vary in such crucial characteristics as age, sex, interests, talents, moods, and needs, find that on frequent occasions they get on each other's nerves, we can be reasonably sure that they are normal members of the human race, expressing universal feelings. Fortunately, what happens to brothers and sisters is the same thing that happens to people in general; being social creatures we find that companionship, friendship, and love offer rich compensations for some of the limitations and frustrations of sharing the world with others. It is silly and pointless to deny the mixed feelings that accompany all close relationships. Our children would be less anxious if we were less self-conscious and fearful. All right, so Junior is jealous; what else is new? That's life! Provided his experiences continue to reinforce his sense of being a loved and valued person in his own right, he will learn to live with his fears and angers, just like the rest of the human race. If we treat it as a fact of life, so will it be.

A related rule is that accepting a fact doesn't mean accepting it in any and all forms. A toddler of two was hitting his baby sister on the head, while the anxious, helpless parents looked on and said, "What can we do? The psychologists are always saying that sibling rivalry is normal."

The very first thing they could do, with all possible speed, is to remove their young son's hand from the place where it's hitting the baby. The baby's relief would be no greater than that of her brother, who is undoubtedly terrified by his uncontrollable impulses and wishes that some reasonably mature adult would come along and stop what he can't stop himself. His guilt at what he knows is wrong will be a far more serious problem than any temporary pangs of jealousy. He needed to be told, "Yes, you're mad at the baby and that's OK, but you can't hurt her any more than we would let a big five-year-old hit you. If you're feeling mad you can say so, or you can bang with a hammer or hit your rag doll; human victims are off limits." There is a vast difference between accepting feelings and accepting acts, and in no life situation are we ever justified in tolerating downright cruelty and injustice.

A twelve-year-old was taunting her younger brother who was failing in fourth-grade arithmetic. When their mother overheard this, she stormed into the room in righteous wrath and said, "You can call him a jerk, you can tell him he's a crumb, but you are not permitted to hurt his feelings about something that he really cares about." That seems to be about the right distinction.

As in all ambivalent relationships (are there any other kind?) the building of life experiences, the development of common associations, added to the not-infrequent joys of comradeship, build an inner core of affection and genuine devotion. The third rule for survival is to have some plain old-fashioned faith in these experiences and in the fundamental qualities of generosity and kindness, sensitivity and compassion, which are just as normal and instinctual as are hate and cruelty.

A charming college girl, in describing herself and her younger brother, observed, "I discovered Les for the first time after I'd been away at school and came home for a visit. He's really quite an interesting person when you get to know him!" Or the comment of a young man who said, "One day my sister and I were reminiscing about our childhood. It was a shock to both of us to discover all the common memories we shared. In a way they were memories that no other two people in the world could have. It made us feel very close." Exhortations on brotherly love cannot produce these feelings. They come when we trust ourselves and our children enough to permit all kinds of feelings to come through.

Two friends were trying to talk to each other on the phone one day and it became increasingly difficult for them to hear each other because of the bedlam of background noise coming from one end of the line. As the volume increased, mother explained that Ricky and Andy, her eight- and eleven-year olds were on the warpath. The friend heard Ricky, reaching the end of his rope, screaming, "I hate him, I hate him, I'm going to kill him!" His mother calmly replied, "All right, so you hate him. But do it more quietly, I'm on the phone."

This seems to represent a sound philosophical acceptance of the necessity of conflict in the lives of our children. Chances are this ready permission to hate at certain appropriate moments (if not too loudly) will give Ricky the encouragement to express those equally frequent and natural responses of love and affection.

The Man in Your Daughter's Life

A mother sent her friend a postcard from a very elegant French restaurant; it read, "My husband is here with a beautiful young blonde. They're so wrapped up in each other, they haven't even noticed that I'm following them." The friend was amused, not appalled, for she knew exactly who the blonde was. She had already been briefed that the "other woman" in this lady's life was her thirteen-year-old daughter!

That was a lucky adolescent girl; the permission, even the encouragement, to have a flirtation with Dad may very well have as much to do with her future relations with the opposite sex as anything else that has happened to her. This is her testing ground; the safe place where she can make her first experiments with being a woman.

There seems to be a growing awareness of the crucial role that fathers play in the lives of their children—and this seems especially so in relation to adolescents. However, many fathers seem to find themselves tongue-tied with daughters. With boys, some lines of communication remain open in terms of common interests, but many fathers who were able to dote affectionately over their daughters at two and three find themselves embarrassed and uncomfortable in relating to teen-age daughters. Many fathers relinquish their role at this point and let Mom take over completely. We find, however, that guidance counselors who work with adolescent girls see a strong correlation between a variety of behavioral difficulties and the lack of a strong relationship with father. Providing the wherewithal for buying clothes, letting mother make all the decisions, refusing to play "the heavy" when necessary, seems to encourage some daughters down the garden path to early dating, late nights out, and premature sexual experimentation.

It is perfectly true that in *Life with Father* days, fathers did not spend a great deal of time with their young daughters—but they *did* represent law and values and they usually had the last word in the selection of proper clothes, parties, friends, and schools. While Mother may have taken care of the details, it was perfectly clear to daughter that Father was in charge.

With the coming of more informal and less authoritarian relationships between parents and children, fathers often seem to have lost far more than they gained—and so have their daughters. There is a growing awareness that what children of all ages and both sexes need from their fathers is not palship but parenthood, not indulgence but standards and expectations. If you have to be a pal to a teen-age daughter, you may feel ill at ease and uncertain; it is hard to see what the rules are in this relationship. On the other hand, a father who knows he is very much in control and who enjoys a genuine sense of authority can be courtly and flirtatious and still very much a father.

Daughters show us in hundreds of ways how desperately they want the safety of controls, the comfort of a man in charge. One twelve-year-old had a running battle with her father every single week on whether or not she was to be allowed to watch a TV program that her father felt was often too sadistic and sensational. Each week he would look at the description of the current segment and make his decision; often he said no simply because he had the very strong impression his daughter was pleased by the protectiveness involved. Each week when she was told she couldn't watch it, she screamed and cried and carried on—and lapped it up. One week she went to visit a friend for the weekend. Much to her father's astonishment, she called home to ask permission to watch the program that week. Father dutifully looked it up and said it was OK. "How would I have ever known whether she watched it or not?" he naïvely asked his wife. "And how would she know she had a father who loved her if you didn't?" his wife answered.

Approval and interest help adolescent girls through a very difficult period of growth. Those who can't get Father to help them find out what it is to be a girl move more quickly into the arena of life; they are less sure who and what they are and will become, and so they seek out boys who they hope can help them figure it all out. They do not yet know how to behave or what to expect; they know nothing of the give and take in boy-girl relationships, and in many cases they and the boys are little help to each other in figuring it all out or in gaining genuine confidence and increasing maturity from the experience.

"What a young girls needs is a forty-two-year-old boy friend," one psychiatrist quipped. "You know, we have always made much of the importance of the relationship between little girls with their fathers—you know, when they are about three to five. That is when 'daddy's little girl' begins to learn about love and being feminine, and it is even more important in early adolescence. A father can let his daughter know that she is truly loved and admired, that she is worthy of respect and genuine affection and should settle for nothing less."

Girls who are encouraged to take it slow and easy in boy-girl relationships often seem vastly relieved; they are quite content with fantasies of romance in which they behave perfectly and are absolutely safe from harm! If Daddy is available to help you feel like a girl, you are able to postpone those relationships for which you aren't really ready.

Walking down a street one day, a father explained to his thirteen-year-old daughter that when he was alone with her, he walked next to the sidewalk, but when another woman was along, then the man walked in the middle. "It is part of a nice old tradition that men want to protect women," he said. "I guess you're teaching me my boyetti-quette," his daughter replied.

A fourteen-year-old girl was going through the throes of a lost love. She had met a young man at camp and was flattered by his attentions, although deep down she had some misgivings about him. When he rejected her some-what cruelly (in his own ineptness and uncertainty) and her mother tried to be solicitous, she said, "It's OK, I'll get over it. Daddy says I'm 'walking proud.' " Her mother commented, "Nothing but an older man's approval could have given her such a look of dignity!"

Teen-age girls who feel safe flirting with their fathers need some help from their mothers as well. Far-fetched as it may sound to the uninitiated, middle-aged ladies can be pretty jealous of the lovely young things that go floating about the house looking Bardot-ish! One mother said, "When Debbie got to need a bigger bra than me, I was crushed!" When a daughter is flirting with her father, she needs to know two things: Daddy will *never* forget for one moment that she's still his little girl (whatever *her* fantasies may be, they are perfectly safe!), and Mother is not really threatened by this "ménage à trois"—she is willing to permit a new and special privacy between her daughter and her husband, but is perfectly capable of demanding her husband back and of maintaining the pri-vacy and romance of her marriage.

One of the most interesting observations parents have been making is that the traditional cold war (and not always so cold, either!) between teen-age daughters and their mothers is not necessarily as inevitable as tomorrow's dawn. One father observed, "I used to come home at night and listen to my wife complain about how fresh and impossible Janet was, and I couldn't understand it—she seemed very sweet and reasonable to me. Later on, when I began acting like a father—showing some interest in her homework, backing up my rules with some authority— she turned all her venom on me, and boy, did *I* find out what my wife meant! Now that I'm getting my share of the cross-fire my wife and Janet have some great times together!" The more we observe teen-age youngsters, the more we discover that when Daddy is playing a strong and active role in his daughter's life, and making her feel womanly, mother and daughter have a better chance of enjoying each other—often to the surprise of both!

Many adolescent girls, feeling more confident in their own growth, made to feel that being a girl is going to be just fine, thank you, show this comfortable self-confidence in enjoying Mother's company more. On one companionable shopping spree, a fourteen-year-old talked her mother into buying a very daring and youthful dress. She kept insisting, "Daddy will love it—I know his taste!"

A successful flirtation means that while Daddy is very much interested in new clothes, ideas about boys, and other vital matters—and even caters to the special interests and preferences once in awhile—he never loses his own standards. One father said, "Once in awhile I buy Ellen a rock and roll record or some bubble gum just to let her know I respect her feelings and interests—but she knows all hell will break loose if I ever *hear* that record playing within my range or see any gum-chewing when I'm around!"

What is good for middle-aged ladies is good for teen-aged girls; they crave the same occasional spoiling, the same catering, but it doesn't have to lead to overindulgence. One father was highly amused when his thirteen-year-old asked him to bring her a cold drink while she was watching television. He started to tell her to go get her own drink and then thought better of it. His daughter had heard him grumbling and groaning about his wife, who always sat down and then remembered something she wanted—and how, despite his complaining, he did the gentlemanly thing, most of the time. "As long as it doesn't become a habit," he grumbled. As he left the room, his daughter looked knowingly at her mother, giggled conspiratorially, and said, "Isn't he impossible?"

Girls who have this fling with their fathers bring to dating a kind of self-knowledge and self-acceptance they could never learn from their contemporaries. Fathers are grown-up men, not scared little boys, utterly bewildered and overcome by little girls. They have a certain *savoir-faire*: being married, we may assume they know *something* about making a woman feel special and cherished!

Father cannot help his daughter unless Mother really permits it to happen. It cannot be "I wash my hands of you—let Daddy worry," and it cannot be Mother always behind the scenes, manipulating and controlling the situation. She must really encourage Father to be himself, to do what he enjoys, say what he thinks, respond in his own way. One young woman recalled, "My father used to take me to the theater once in a while, but I always knew that my mother was the one who bought the tickets and told him to take me. It wasn't his idea—and anyway, the things he might have done with me were different from what my mother chose, so it didn't count."

The girl who boasts, "I'm so lucky, my father lets me do anything I want," is really envious of the youngster who says, "My father drives me wild—he has to approve of every piece of clothing I buy!" One mother said that she had allowed her thirteen-year-old to buy a pair of shoes with semi-high heels. All the way home her daughter kept groaning, "Daddy will *kill* me, when he sees these heels! He'll just *die*—you *know* he doesn't let me wear heels." She was greatly disappointed when father didn't even notice—and utterly delighted when he growled and carried on, after she'd called it to his attention!

The gains are not all to the girls. "I had to make an effort at first," one father admitted. "And for a long time I thought I was just doing something necessary for my child's happiness. Then one day she turned me down when I suggested we do something together and I found myself feeling very rejected! I hate to admit it, but it's very pleasant dating a lovely young female who obviously appreciates all your sterling qualities!"

That inevitable day *does* come—and fathers must gird themselves for it—when gradually the younger men move into the forefront. They may take what comfort they can from such comments as these: A fifteen-year-old observed to her mother one day, "Isn't it peculiar—have you noticed how many of the boys I like look like Daddy?" And a sixteen-year-old confided to her mother, "Have you noticed we like the same types of men?"

Where Preschoolers
Take Their Problems

After watching nursery-age children for many years, I've come to the conclusion that one can tell a good deal about their mental health by where they take their troubles.

When a mother comes in for a conference at the nursery school and stares at us, dumbfounded, when we tell her what a joy her child is, we have discovered that usually we are right in being quite optimistic about his development, even though she soon tells us hair-raising stories about his behavior at home. This child, whom we see willingly sharing the only working bicycle with a friend, always ready to help at clean-up time, has a very different pattern at home. In fact his mother is ready to cut her throat, she tells us, because he hits the baby, gets paint on the wallpaper, screams bloody murder when it's bath time, and won't go to sleep until his parents are staggering with fatigue. Whatever is bothering him, he sure is managing to leave it at home when, eagerly and happily, he climbs into the school station-wagon.

Then there is the opposite situation in which we might call both parents into school because we are so upset about a child's behavior. The temper tantrums are piling up, and we see great anxiety often preceded by furious anger at teachers and children; we are more and more concerned about a child who seems to have less and less tolerance for frustration and seems to us to be pretty miserable a good part of the time. This child's parents look at each other in speechless shock. Can we really be talking about *their* child? It can't be possible! At home he is a paragon of virtue—polite, helpful, and obedient. We find ourselves as teachers and counselors becoming uncomfortable and defensive. We know that it is more than likely that on the way home these parents will begin to talk about switching to another nursery school. What kind of crazy place is this where people go around looking for problems?

By and large—and of course with many exceptions—a child who shows unhappy behavior at home but does beautifully in school is likely to come out of whatever problems he may be having far more easily than the child who is having problems at school but behaves like an angel at home. We have now followed up literally hundreds of these situations and the consistency of this observation is quite startling.

I think there is a good reason for this—at least one that seems logical to me. At the age of three or four, whatever hang-ups you've got are the result of what is happening to you in the bosom of your family; that's where the psychological action is. If you are a pretty sturdy, healthy little kid and if you feel reasonably secure that your parents love you a lot, then you are likely to have the courage it takes to fight whatever you've got to fight about right there, where it's happening. If you can't stand the new baby, you let everybody know about it. If your dumb mother doesn't see that you're getting bigger and should have more autonomy, you raise all kinds of hell when she tries to boss you around. You work on your problems right where they're happening because you're not afraid to take that chance.

If, on the other hand, you are pretty scared and tentative, and getting the love and approval you need can't always be counted on, then home is not a very good place to show how you feel. You try hard to cover up what's bothering you because you don't dare to upset the family emotional applecart—but you have to unburden yourself *somewhere*, so you dump your pain and frustration onto your friends and teachers. Maybe they will love you, anyway—but if they don't, well, they aren't as important as your parents. Let *them* see your misery or wrath—but keep that stiff upper lip around the house.

There is something quite healthy about a child's trying to work out his problems in the appropriate place and having enough sense of reality to use school for it's own kind of growing.

If a nursery school report suggests very unusual and intense acting-out behavior, I'd first want to be sure that the report was reliable: How long has it been observed? How experienced are the teachers observing it? What kind of atmosphere is there in the classroom in general? Then I'd want to take another look at what may be some well-hidden concerns that ought to be handled on the home front. If, on the other hand, your preschooler is driving you out of your mind at home but is doing just fine in school, you may take some comfort—as you try to roll with the punches—in knowing that your child knows just where his problem must be solved and isn't afraid to get on with it.

Social Life
in the Grades

We were visiting some friends recently, and Linda, the fifteen-year-old in the family, came into the living room briefly. She was barefoot, wearing blue jeans and one of her father's old torn shirts. Her mother commented, "When she was ten, all she wanted out of life was a pair of stockings, a lipstick, and high-heeled shoes. At this advanced age of fifteen, she wouldn't be caught dead with any of these items, now freely available to her."

For those harassed parents whose youngsters are still in grade school but who see themselves as sophisticated men and women of the world, ready for dating and kissing, let us—the aged who have lived through this phase—encourage you to take heart. We have news for you: that nine-year-old who pleads for the padded A-cup bra will in a few years hide any and all evidences of her gender under a size-40 sweater; that eleven-year-old who wants to take his girl friend to the movie (at *night*!) will discover at fourteen that he is terrified at the possibilities inherent in a two-sex world, and for some time his trips to movies, basketball games, and bowling alleys will become strictly stag.

What is this strange reversibility all about? I think we can find a very good clue in our observations of four- and five-year olds. Watch any doll corner in any nursery school and you will see four-year-old girls feeding and burping other four-year-old girls, and five-year-old boys running the fire department or going to the office "to make more money." *We* know it's just dramatic play, so we don't give it a second thought. If we knew just how serious and important this play-acting was to those children, we might be just as nervous about their social sophistication as we are about the fifth-graders who want to dance and have kissing games. Certainly four-year-olds are not old enough to be mothers and fathers, and yet they want to wear our shoes and hats and carry our pocketbooks—and too often they sound painfully like us, especially when they are "yelling at the children"! For many years we have recognized that one of the very best ways in which children learn about the roles they will someday play is through imitation—the practice of dramatic play. I would like to suggest that the social antics of our grade-school children are really dramatic play. They are more interested in mommies and daddies at four—so that's what they want to practice to be. At ten you are more interested in those dim, strange, frightening, and exciting years that lie ahead—those years in which your body will go through the strange and mysterious metamorphosis taking you from childhood to adulthood; those years when you will find your place as a boy or girl in relation to other boys and girls; those years when you will be learning what it really is to be a man or a woman.

It is too late to practice when you get there. Then you are caught up in a whirlpool of physiological and psychological changes, and you know that what happens between males and females is dynamite. It is much better to "study" about all this before you ever get there—before you're close enough to understand and feel it too well. Wearing two-inch heels at twelve, manfully suggesting a fast game of spin-the-bottle at eleven—these are ways of testing what's ahead before one is emotionally involved. At fifteen or sixteen it's too late to practice—someone is more than likely to take you seriously. At this more advanced age most young people are scared to death of each other because now they know exactly how loaded, how explosive, their relations to each other can become.

In recent years parents have been increasingly concerned about the pseudo-sophistication of young children— the early dating and partying, the fancy and expensive clothes, the elaborate birthday parties, etc. Some of their anxiety has been justified; some of it seems excessive.

Let us imagine, for example, that your child is again three years old, instead of nine or ten. She has invited several little friends in to play on a cold winter afternoon. You notice that they are playing house and are having a tea party; instead of asking them if they'd like some "real cocoa" in the doll teacups, you call up your husband at the office and tell him to reserve a table at a fancy restaurant that specializes in afternoon tea. You say, "Susan wants a tea party, what can we do?"

This seems in many cases to be what we do with our pre-teens: we observe their natural tendency to mimic and to play-act, and we take it seriously and behave in ways that are completely inappropriate. Sometimes we are using our children for our own social purposes; sometimes we fulfill some old and ought-to-be-dead-and-buried fantasies of our own. This is especially true when we recall our own adolescence with discomfort, when we remember our ineptness and our suffering. One mother told me, "When I realized what we had spent on Donna's twelfth birthday party—a catered Luau, no less—I began to wonder if I was trying to relive *my* adolescence and make it all glamorous and wonderful. All I remember is acne and being a wall flower—and I think I was trying to undo those memories."

It is when we parents enter into the game, support it by overindulgence or extravagance, encourage and titilate, that it gets out of hand. Sensible expression of one's understanding, and controlled and guided social activities, even though they seem unchildlike and therefore foolish and unnecessary, won't hurt at all and seem to be needed by children in their exploration of the world that lies before them. Giving a ten-year-old girl one or two pairs of stockings that she can wear on very special occasions, letting a twelve-year-old use a little makeup, not only will fail to corrupt her, but this may be the only year she'll use the stuff until she's over twenty-one! Permitting youngsters to have boy-girl parties and allowing them to go to dancing classes will also not corrupt if parents play their own entirely appropriate role as guides and guardians. Simple parties with lots of well-planned games and social dancing classes with mature experienced teachers and lots of good sound rules that make it fun for everybody, not just for the most popular and beautiful, are ways in which our children test themselves for what they dimly (and often entirely inaccurately!) see ahead. For some reason we have tended to be far less sensible about our role and function at this age than we were when our children were younger. If Johnny at four said he was a fireman, we didn't buy him a fire house—we bought him a toy engine; if four-year-old Nancy wanted to be a mother, we didn't leave home and let her take over—we bought her a doll that could drink and wet its pants. In exactly the same way, when our nines to twelves come up with grandiose plans for taking the gang to a nightclub or having a party in which all the grown-ups go out to the movies, we don't have to do it! Most of our present anxiety and concern is because some foolish parents did, and once the lid was off, our children's natural impulses bloomed far and wide. It is possible to permit children to pretend they are what they are not without making it unnatural, excessive, and even dangerous.

One mother found that she could let her twelve-year-old daughter play at being a lady in a very harmless and inexpensive way for her birthday celebration. Judy invited five of her closest friends to have lunch in a restaurant and to go to a movie, alone, downtown. The restaurant, selected ahead of time, had an excellent Chow Mein Special every Saturday for $2.25, and there was an appropriate movie nearby. What was most important was that the girls used public transportation rather than being chauffered by their parents. In our suburban world, this is one of the heaviest burdens of infantilization our children bear; city kids are on their own at a much earlier age, and if and when we *can* give a youngster an opportunity for getting places on his own, this has tremendous significance for him. By prearrangement all the mothers had agreed that the young ladies could wear stockings and heels and some lipstick; probably the girls put more on when they were on their own! It was a glorious afternoon of pretending to be grown-up—and we need to respect the need for this "practice."

We need to be able to give certain permissions without losing control, without becoming as unrealistic as our children may be inclined to become. In addition, when we permit a child to experiment with being older, we need to make it clear that this may impress *him,* but not *us.* The problem in the social acceleration of children is that most kids probably always knew it wasn't for real, but their parents often acted as if it was. If ten-year-old Patty desperately wants some false eyelashes, having them isn't going to destroy her moral fiber. If she gets them but is told it's only for once in awhile and it's pretty silly anyhow, at least she knows that her parents haven't forgotten her chronological age—they're just being kind. If, on the other hand we suggest that a youngster buy a corsage for a girl he is taking to the school dance, if we buy insanely expensive party dresses, if we talk about how popular our child is with the opposite sex—if, indeed, we get seduced into our child's dreams, then we are not acting like parents and we soon see the loss of control, the hedonism, the cynicism, of our youth, who know so well when we stop taking care of them.

Several years ago there was an uproar in one affluent suburban community when a mother participated in the kissing games at her eleven-year-old son's party. Her mistaken and misguided idea was that if she could show what a pal she was, the children wouldn't feel they had to do things behind her back. She "timed" the kisses in a closet to which each boy and girl went in the course of the game. It is this kind of abdication from parental responsibility that has given kissing games a bad name!

Pseudo-sophisticated antics are all right so long as grownups don't take them seriously—so long as they don't forget the age and the real immaturity of the child. Things won't get out of hand if children recognize that there are limits and if they are comforted by the clear knowledge that even though parents may permit attendance at a dancing class, they still know you want to be fed when

you're sick, and even if they give you a lipstick for
Christmas, they know that you still need your broken-
down old teddy bear to go to sleep with. If *we* keep our
heads, our children will know how old they really are,
whatever their dreams may be.

Homosexuality

Two more highly publicized books on homosexuality
have appeared recently to join the gathering mass of
material on this subject. One book breaks with tradition
and blames fathers for making homosexuals out of their
sons, the other book sticks with the psychoanalytic
catechism that it's all Mom's fault. I am disturbed by the
fact that such books, expressing so little humility—so sure
they know exactly what they are talking about—are likely
to frighten a great many parents of young children and
leave parents of homosexuals flooded with irreparable
feelings of guilt. It seems to me that we are not in any
position to be so sure about how parent-child relationships
effect a child's sexual orientation.

Most psychiatric approaches to homosexuality have as-
serted that it is brought about during the first three or
four years of life by the attitudes and behavior of one or
both parents. There are a variety of descriptions of how
parents behaved, but the judgments seem somewhat im-
prudent to me since I have never yet read or heard a case
history without being able to think of at least ten other
families with similar characteristics where the boy children
managed to become heterosexual males very nicely, thank
you. Why some kids and not others? No analyst has ever
answered this to my satisfaction or to that of a growing
minority of psychologists and psychiatrists who are taking
a new look at this subject.

Psychiatric theory to date has also assumed that homosexuality is pathological—that it is a disease. Before

one accepts this assumption it seems reasonable to ask how come homosexuality was accepted so completely during some of the high moments in man's cultural history? If it is a disease, why didn't it ruin these societies? There is general agreement that one of the proudest and most creative periods in human history occurred in Greece in about 450 B.C., when homosexuality was viewed as merely one of many acceptable ways to love.

Humanistic and existential psychotherapists, representing a new group breaking with much of psychoanalytic tradition, are beginning to view pathology—mental illness— in different terms: as something that interferes with or actively destroys an individual's capacity to fulfill himself, to live creatively with himself and others. In this light, one would not make judgments on the basis of sexual orientation, but rather on whether or not this part of one's life worked for or against personal fulfillment and enhanced or impeded one's capacity for continuing growth. If we were to judge the degree of psychological pathology by the sexually inventive and highly individual tastes and pleasures of married heterosexual couples, we'd be in big trouble, because what goes on behind bedroom doors in a marriage relationship is strictly a private matter. If one or both partners are unhappy or emotionally disturbed, their sex life may serve as symptomatic of other troubles, but we would hesitate to say that this is the *cause* of their problems. A newer approach to homosexuality would interest itself not in the fact of the homosexuality itself, but in its place in the life of a particular human being—and the range is just as wide as it would be with heterosexuals: from frightened, destructive, miserable people who have never found themselves, to people who live creatively, constructively, and in mature and responsible love relationships.

The newer breed of therapist asks not whether his patient is homosexual or heterosexual, but whether he has found successful avenues for expressing what is most special and valuable in himself as a human being. From such a point of view, one's sexual preferences become secondary to other questions having to do with an individual's struggle to find his own identity as a person.

Undoubtedly one of the reasons that makes it so easy to view homosexuality as a disease is that, because of social attitudes, the majority of homosexuals seem to have more than their fair share of self-contempt and self-hatred. Anyone who grows up not liking himself is in trouble, and in our society this is the likely fate of most homosexuals.

The danger is great that parents can become self-conscious and uneasy with their children when they read reports on how they influence their children's sexuality. I have seen mothers who are hysterical with fear when their perfectly normal four-year-old sons wanted to wear high heels, and affectionate fathers who are ashamed that they like to have their children climb into bed with them on a Sunday morning. Have a little humility! It isn't really that easy to influence a child's sexual orientation—even if it could be done, it would take herculean efforts of day and night work by terribly determined people! It is important to remember that for every aggressively seductive mother and passive or emotionally absent father whose son turns out to be a homosexual, there are other mothers and fathers with exactly the same qualities who get to be grandmas and grandpas in the traditional fashion. If we do not yet understand the mysterious complexities involved, it seems to me we have a responsibility not to offer inflexible theories to cover our ignorance.

The sensible parent will assume that a fulfilling and satisfying adult life must be based on self-acceptance and that, without concerning oneself with predicting future sexual preferences, the chances are good that a youngster who has a good image of himself is more than likely to become a heterosexual. At least we can say that such a child won't choose deviation or some degree of social separateness because of self-dislike. However, even in a relatively comfortable home, where parents enjoy their own sexuality and have encouraged their children to discover their own talents and possibilities, a child may grow up to prefer homosexual relationships. Does that have to be the end of the world? I am reminded of an earlier day when a patrician mother discovered that her son wanted to be a truck driver, and she said, "All right, if you must—but be the best truck driver you can be." The day may come when, without feeling overwhelming panic and guilt, a parent might be able to say, "Be a homosexual if you prefer, but be the best *person* who is a homosexual that you can possibly be."

Teen-agers
and Discipline

Whatever conclusions one may come to about permissiveness and discipline, it sure is a lot easier to put theory into practice when one's child is too young to really fight back. Misbehavior in a two- or a five- or a nine-year-old may drive us up the wall, but we have some sense of control over the situation.

One of the things that scares us about being the parents of teen-agers is that we feel we can no longer really punish effectively. Older children are away from home so much of the time that it is almost impossible to make a punishment stick. You just can't hire a detective to follow teen-agers wherever they go. There comes a point where you just can't get away with yelling or spanking or isolating, and depriving a youngster just doesn't make any sense because you can't enforce it. Parents get a creepy feeling of helplessness. It's very scary to lose one's Parent Power!

Scary but inevitable. And because it is going to happen, it behooves us to keep it in mind during those earlier years when we *do* have some leeway and control. In deciding on how to discipline a younger child, we must keep in mind that today's teen-agers are not home very much and that they are far more influenced by their peers than by us. If this is so, we ought to do everything possible to try to devise forms of discipline that will provide opportunities for learning the decision-making process—for the development of inner controls based on a child's own successful evaluation of a situation. If, for example, a child is going to be under your thumb until manhood, punishment through fear may work. If, on the other hand, he is going to be buffeted by many winds long before he is an adult, he will need to start much earlier in developing his own good judgment and a system of values that can afford him guidelines in making his own decisions. He will need to know the reasons for things; he will need to feel that he can direct his own life, and that nothing is really more important than how *he* decides what he may or may not allow *himself* to do.

Assuming we work at this kind of self-discipline and try in the early years to impart our philosophy of life, we then have to accept the fact that we are going to have to let go and take our chances. Once a child is thirteen or fourteen, he is going to have to decide whether or not to steal, to take drugs, to destroy other people's property, to cheat in school, to have sex relations. The freedom, the opportunities for getting oneself into trouble, are simply enormous today, and they cannot be avoided. This reality forces us to develop techniques for democratic discipline in the earlier years so that our children may be inner-directed before they face these choices. Once they are adolescents we have to assume that we have done the best we possibly could. Then we have to expect that our children will probably make some pretty serious mistakes in judgment and need our help in solving the resulting problems. We need to prepare ourselves not to overreact or greet each crisis as though the child is deliberately trying to make our lives miserable. There is nothing that is less helpful to a "fallen" teen-ager than to hear a parent say "How could you do this to me?" Whatever sort of mess he's gotten himself into, parental self-pity is no antidote.

We ought to remember that society has become so complex and turbulent that it is almost impossible to have an uneventful adolescence anymore. Our children understand this; they are not shocked by being arrested, for example—something that we see as horrifying and shameful because it never happened to us. In one typical middle-class suburban family where the parents' only contact with the law was an occasional traffic ticket their fourteen-year-old son has twice been arrested. He has long hair and wears beads, and one day he was waiting at a crossroads for his mother to pick him up and drive him to a music lesson when a policeman told him to move on. He asked why, which strikes me as a reasonable question, and was taken to the police station for defying an officer. On another occasion he was involved in a serious prank. He and two other boys took some cars parked in driveways and with keys in them and simply moved them around a bit, so that all the cars were still within four or five blocks of their own driveways, but mixed up. Second encounter with the law. Twenty-five years ago such youthful mischievousness would have been handled by irate parents who would have meted out some appropriately severe punishment—which they could have enforced. In our complicated society it is increasingly likely that our children will become involved with outside law enforcement agencies. We find ourselves having to learn new attitudes: to be grateful and unembarrassed when police intervention is genuinely protective and justified and to assert our authority and not knuckle under when we feel an injustice is being done.

Like it or not, we have lost our total authority and responsibility where young people are concerned. It would seem, therefore, that one of the greatest contributions we could make toward a reasonably secure world for our kids would be to see to it that the community agencies with which they are likely to come in contact are enlightened—that they have an understanding of the stresses and strains of adolescence and the vision and compassion to provide the same kind of reasoned guidance *we* tried to bring to bear in the earlier years.

Healthy and Irritating Signs of Independence

I was talking with a friend on the phone the other day, offering her my sympathy and compassion. She was the distraught mother of two boys, seven and nine years of age, both of whom had been home from school with the flu for two weeks. In addition to reporting on the usual lack of sleep and resulting exhaustion that attend a mother's role as Florence Nightingale, she was full of anecdotes about the boys' hair-raising escapades. After describing some of their more colorful and nerve-shattering activities, she sighed and said, "This much 'togetherness' tries a

mother's soul. They haven't enough to challenge and stimulate their seething little minds, so they are giving me
the works. They're just as defiant and argumentative as
they can be." She paused, then added more cheerfully, "Of
course, the nice thing about fresh kids is that they are so
smart."

That comment has stuck in my mind. I remember a
mother in a parents' discussion group who became very
much upset when the other members complained about
children who defied what their parents felt to be the most
reasonable of controls. She interrupted these tales of woe
with a story that no one in that group will ever forget.

"You know," she said, "it's very hard for me to listen to
you complain. You should be glad your children have such
spirit. I have two children, a boy of eight and a little girl
of four. Paul was a devilish one from the day he was
born. He was always getting into things. He was hard to
discipline. He wore me out. When my little girl was born,
she was entirely different—quiet, passive, uncomplaining.
She was so undemanding and easy to handle that I
thought to myself, "Well, thank goodness, at least I've got
one child who isn't going to be a lot of trouble.' But Carol
didn't seem to develop right. She didn't try to sit up, she
didn't crawl, she didn't play. To make a long story short,
she is a retarded child. Now every time Paul gets hard to
handle, my husband and I thank God that he's a normal
boy, trying to grow up." Though this is an extreme situation, it does point out dramatically and clearly that we
can't have our cake and eat it too.

What do we want our children to be like when they
grow up? Most of the parents I've met seem to agree that
they want their children to be responsible, independent
adults. They want them to be able to make mature decisions about work, marriage, and parenthood. They want
them to be discriminating in their judgment of people and
ideas and to live fully with a sense of adventure, unafraid
to explore the world (even the universe) around them.
They want their children to be flexible enough to accept
change, courageous enough to meet new challenges, loving
and sensitive enough to care deeply about life and about
people.

The catch is that there is no way to achieve these goals
except through the innate human struggle to grow. We

applaud when it gives our children the impetus to learn to walk, speak, eat without help, tie shoelaces, make friends, read and write, add and subtract. But we are often somewhat less enthusiastic about the natural impulse to grow when it shows itself in the form of defiance, stubbornness, toughness toward ourselves, indifference to the rules of cleanliness, and irresponsibility about chores that are important to us but not to them.

I suspect that most of our concerns about discipline, about setting limits and at the same time encouraging independence, center on our natural confusion and uncertainty. How, we ask ourselves, can we help our children become civilized beings yet still allow for the wonderful richness of individual difference and the development of mature independence? Probably the first thing to do is accept the fact that children have to test themselves against adult authority. How do you know what you can do until you try it? Can you always take your parents' word for it that you are not ready for some new experience? Maybe you are and they don't know it.

Most parents recognize that when a child insists on getting his own way and when he goes through the "emancipation acrobatics" typical of children his age, these are evidences of growth. What we have learned about child development has given us a sense of proportion about such transitory, trial-and-error experiments with independence as bad table manners, indifference to neatness, or occasional lying, fighting, tantrums, and defiance.

Certainly the healthy struggle for independence doesn't always take the form of fighting against adult authority. It shows itself in an eagerness for learning, in rapture over opportunities to increase physical skills, in a valiant struggle for acceptance among one's own friends. When experiences at school and at home encourage self-confidence and pride in real accomplishments, children find many avenues for self-development.

Intense and continuous rebellion is something else again. When the irritating signs of independence outweigh the positive ones, we may need to ask a few questions. Are we getting an inordinate amount of defiance because our controls are too stiff? Are we giving eight-year-old Johnny no more freedom than we gave him at five? Or have we gone so far to the other extreme that ten-year-old

Judy's constant rebellious behavior is really a plea for more limits, because she isn't ready to handle the choices we are giving her? Is Fred just being ornery in his stubborn refusal to wear that pair of slacks, or will he really lose face with his friends if he does?

As adults we have a right to set limits when children are too immature to control their own antisocial impulses. We are responsible for their safety and well-being; we must safeguard them from real dangers when they are too young and inexperienced to protect themselves or one another. Most important of all, we are responsible for serving as living examples of what we believe. Yet we also need to allow children to be children. We tell them what we believe and what we expect, but we give them years and years in which to measure up to adult standards.

Assuming that the unlovely behavior we see in most growing children is natural, do we have to resign ourselves to living with it? Most seasoned parents will say, "Yes, at least some of the time." But this is not the whole story. There are lots of things we can do to make life reasonably pleasant for ourselves as well as our children, permitting growth but at the same time maintaining sound and satisfying human relationships. We can choose our ground. It takes two to tangle!

Parents make such choices all day long. As one mother put it: "For weeks I had been nagging Jeff about hanging up his pajamas and bathrobe and making his bed. One day when he didn't do it, I was so mad that the minute he came home from school I started yelling. I realized later that he had come in with a big smile, gay and happy, eager to tell me something, but when I started bawling him out he went to his room, banged the door shut, did his chores, and hardly spoke to me during dinner. Next day I found out he had been elected class president and had run all the way home to tell me about it. Suddenly I asked myself, Which is more important, to get mad when he doesn't do his chores or to be his friend? I still have to remind him every day about cleaning up, but love is more important than pajamas on the floor."

Which things must we insist on and which are really not that important? A quiet, companionable game or a lecture on table manners? A spic-and-span house or an atmosphere of affection and well-being? A father once told me,

"When I was a kid, my mother always had a big, formal chicken dinner on Sunday. I grew up feeling that this was terribly important, and when my wife preferred greater informality, I felt that we were missing out on a family ritual. But now that our children are almost grown, I realize we have had some wonderful Sundays together: spur-of-the-moment picnics, munching on hamburgers, or maybe just loafing, reading, and talking—all of us together. I told my wife she was right. I hardly ever saw my mother on Sundays. She was too busy cooking that chicken dinner!"

Another thing we can do is respect our children's work. There is less need to prove you are growing up if the people around you seem to know it. When the family sits down to dinner, how often do the children get a chance to tell about their day? As a charter member of the guilty club, I can remember many conversations centered on the trials, tribulations, challenges, and successes of my husband's day or mine but not very many about our daughter's. Do we let our children know that growing up, learning new skills, working at becoming an accepted member of one's group is really a hard job? And that we respect and admire this task enough to realize that children too are often discouraged and tired as well as excited and triumphant at the end of the day?

"Accentuating the positive" is another attitude that can be helpful. Our children would have to be deaf, dumb, and blind not to know what we dislike about their behavior, but how often do we tell them how proud we are of their successes? Do we praise the signs of growth that impress us so enormously? And above all, when they are behaving in the most exasperating or impossible ways, are they aware that we know they really want to be liked, want to behave well? Children can feel pretty awful about what they do or say. They know they are being childish, silly, naughty, but they can't seem to help it. Why not reassure them by pointing out that childishness is pretty logical when you are a child, that we realize they are constantly struggling to become more grown up and that it takes a lot of practice and hard work.

Humor is another asset in living with the irritating aspects of growth. When Ronnie comes home, mimicking his tough pals by answering our requests with, "So what?

You can't make me!" or "You wanna bet?" or "That's tough on you!" or more unprintable words of emancipation, we can get huffy, we can get stern, we can moralize or punish—or we can joke about it. "Boy, aren't *we* getting tough!" said with a wry smile, carries as much of a message as a lot of parental sermons—perhaps more.

Sometimes we are so fearful of losing control over children that we get too serious and intent about superficial and insignificant evidences of the struggle for independence. We can often make it clear to children that we "get the message" with a laugh or a joke or a game of words instead of a scowl and a command. No child that I know ever saw this as an abdication of adult authority, a wishy-washy permissiveness to do whatever he pleased. Quite the contrary. Our children know very well that they are children and that we grown-ups handle the reins. That's why they defy us.

Most of the children we live with admire and respect us. They want, eventually, to be like us. They know perfectly well what we stand for, what we believe to be the essentials for decent human relationships. They are nice, normal, healthy, wonderful—though annoying and provoking—children who have to test us and themselves, who have to feel and act like children, who have to learn, slowly but steadily, inner controls and sensible self-expression. They drive us crazy, but they are also enchanting. In spite of the torn jacket, the unbrushed teeth, the forgotten chore, the restless feet that keep our shins black and blue at the dining-room table, they will surprise us by rallying to an emergency, showing tact and sensitivity in a complicated relationship, working out a difficult and original science club project, getting sentimental and slushy about last summer's family camping trip.

Concern over the apparent increase in antisocial behavior among youngsters is clearly warranted; hysterical, undocumented warnings of doom for all lively children are not. When Junior talks back and the next-door neighbor's eyebrows go up, keep a sense of proportion. Junior is not a deprived, hurt child—hungry for recognition and affection, for the stability and security of a loving family and likely to become seriously delinquent. He is *your child*, someone who knows you love and respect him, who has a deep sense of the interdependence of mutual need and love. This sometimes rebellious, often sloppy and forgetful, occasionally really naughty boy, will some day be a mature, responsible "doctor, lawyer, Indian chief." He will take his place in society as a civilized human being, giving and getting love and affection, having an inner sense of direction and purpose.

What's more, that younger sister of his—the one in blue jeans who loses her mittens, forgets to feed the dog, refuses to help with the dishes, and can't sit still, the one whose hair is always flying in all directions—she's going to be an excellent homemaker, wife and mother, community worker. One day these two and their respective future spouses will be PTA members, and undoubtedly they will be asking the guest speaker at a regular monthly PTA meeting, "What can we do? Our children are so fresh, so messy, so noisy, so defiant. How can we make them behave?"

The Under-deprived Child

A health expert recently caused quite a commotion by suggesting that school bus transportation only be provided for children living two or more miles from school. It was his thesis that the nation's children would be in far better physical shape if they had to walk to school and that at least 50 percent of the chauffering now being done by parents was unnecessary coddling.

At first glance one is inclined to think of these nonwalking children as overprivileged; in one sense they are—there is too much car in their lives. But in another sense they are deprived—of the robust good health and the feelings of freedom and independence that might well come from doing more of their locomoting on their own. In other words, many of our most privileged children are under-deprived: given too many *things*, they have little opportunity to experience some of the important feelings and events that are essential to healthy maturation. If we deprived them of too easy and quick comfort, if we deprived them of the excessive quantity of toys that they drown in, if we deprived them of the immediate gratification of every wish, we might well be finally giving them what they *really* need—a chance to search out solutions to problems, an opportunity to feel the deep and gratifying self-respect that comes with achieving one's goals by oneself.

Under-deprived youngsters rarely if ever know the exquisite joy of waiting for something, of anticipating and dreaming, nor do they discover the pride in working for a difficult goal on their own.

One mother reported that she recently went through the horrors of spring cleaning in her adolescent daughter's room. "I suddenly saw clearly how lack of 'deprivation' can give a child such a false sense of values. In that room there was a broken sewing machine; it had been bought by doting grandparents for a twelfth birthday and had been used for making one dress and then never used again. There was a guitar, bought over a year ago and accompanied by a year's lessons with an excellent teacher. When the teacher moved away and one string broke, it was never played again. A record player had needed a new needle for several months and was gathering dust on the closet floor next to a typewriter given as a Christmas gift two years before, when my daughter swore that she needed one desperately for her school work. She had never taken the trouble to learn to use it. Then there was the newest acquisition, a tape recorder, left uncovered, the tapes scrambled in complete disorder.

"I found myself feeling sick at the waste, furious at my child, and suddenly aware of how foolish I had been to permit this. We aren't rich people, and the money for all these luxuries could have been used for other needs. Even if we had been millionaires, we should never have let our daughter develop such bad attitudes toward possessions. I began to wonder how she would ever stand the normal frustrations of life as an adult when she had almost never waited for anything she wanted as a child."

Several years ago a leading psychiatrist stated that one reason for the increasing number of very early marriages among middle class youngsters while still in college (to say nothing of earlier sexual experimentation) was that we seemed to be in the process of raising a generation who never quite gave up demand feeding. From birth, these children were taught that they never had to wait for the fulfillment of any gratification—they had a right to anything they wanted when they wanted it. While self-demand feeding may be appropriate in infancy, our apparent adaptation of this concept to much later periods of growth has deprived our children of the normal and realistic experiences of frustration, of struggle, of waiting for—and enjoying more—the fruits of responsible labor.

When we give our children too many things, we are in a sense saying to them, "We don't have much faith in you at all; if we don't supply you with a great many toys, you won't be able to think of anything to do. If we don't give you fancy clothes and cars at age sixteen, you won't feel loved. You are too weak and too infantile to endure waiting for things you want, or working for them." We are saying that we are afraid of our children. A father commented recently, "I don't know a single parent who really believes, deep down, that any sixteen-year-old really has the experience in living or the emotional maturity to be allowed to own a car or even to drive one without supervision, no matter how good his technical skills may be; and yet we are giving them cars, and some of them are being maimed for life, even killed. Are we afraid to let them be mad at us? Is this being a *parent?*"

Certainly we cannot blame under-deprivation of our children on the affluent society; wealthy families throughout history have often been the most stern and demanding with their children. Is it our own memories of the Depression? Are we giving our children things that were denied us? Is it part of our confusion about values and standards in facing the complexities and anxieties of the world we live in? Is it in part a lazy abdication from making demands or having expectations that involve enduring our children's disapproval and anger? Undoubtedly it is many things, but we had better take note of what we are doing. We are keeping our children in cotton batting both physically and emotionally.

We show our fear and our lack of respect for the strength and resilience in our children in many ways, not only in what we give them. One father told me that he and his wife went through agonies of guilt when they decided to move from the suburbs into the city. He said, "I had *had* it with the commuting, and decided that my exhaustion and irritability were worse for my wife and kids than giving up the back yard and the suburban school. But once we made the decision, we were terrified: What if the children were unhappy? Suppose they didn't make new friends? Suppose they hated the new school? How could they stand not being able to play outdoors anytime they felt like it? We went to see the school guidance counselor and she really shocked us. She said, 'Have a little respect for your children. Give them the right to discover that they *can* accept the challenge—don't deprive them of that good feeling.' She was right; it was tough for awhile, but we didn't slobber over them or let them wallow in self-pity, and they made it eventually— with real pride."

A mother recently told me that her teen-age daughter offered to bring her breakfast in bed on a Sunday morning. "I started to say 'No, don't bother,' and suddenly realized I was making a mistake. My daughter's face clouded and she said, 'Can't you ever let *me* do something for *you*?'" Young people need opportunities to feel that they are helping and giving to others; when they have none of these experiences, they cannot discover their own strength and durability; they cannot have the self-respect that comes with knowing that you are a good person helping others.

Another mother reminisced, "I had just heard my father had had a heart attack, and I burst into tears. Suddenly I found myself enveloped, resting my head on a warm and ample young breast. *I* could take strength and comfort from my sixteen-year-old daughter—what a wonderful feeling it was! It was weeks later before I realized what my need of her had meant to her. She knew that she had been a tower of strength in a crisis, and she walked with a new dignity and self-confidence. Giving her my *need* had done more for her than all the things and privileges that we had heaped on her."

All children have a right to be needed, to know that they must contribute to the family, that they must take on increasing responsibilities for the well-being of the family. They need to know that they must give, not merely be given to. They have the right to find out how marvelous it feels to struggle through a problem and solve it. A mother reports, "When Kathy, our fifteen-year-old, was invited to a special dance, she asked us to help her find jobs for which she could earn some money. She walked dogs, set hair, did some clerical work—and on her own, bought a new outfit. Her pleasure in it was very special. Every person has a right to struggle to achieve his own goals." A teen-age boy was offered a car for his seventeenth birthday. He explained to his grandmother why he didn't want it, despite the fact that Grandpa could well afford this gift. He told her, "I'll enjoy it more if I have to earn it myself in the next couple of years."

Our misguided wish to give more than is needed in material possessions means that we give less of what is *really* needed—an opportunity to behave responsibly and earn one's own self-respect. Our young people crave such experiences—and when they cannot tell us so as directly and as sensibly as this young man, it is up to us as adults to control our impulses to be over-generous and over-protective. We need to "deprive" our children of those things that interfere with healthy struggle and challenge. We need to have enough faith and self discipline to permit our children to grow up.

What Children Know About Parents

It was a Saturday morning and I was furious with myself for having put off my shopping until the worst of all possible times. The supermarket was crowded and I was waiting on a long line to have some bananas weighed when I heard a child calling from another part of the store, "Daddy, Daddy, where *are* you?" A tall, attractive man absorbed in checking a shopping list looked up, annoyed, and shouted in an angry voice, "I'm over *here!*" Without the least show of interest or concern for his child's whereabouts, he proceeded to put some pears into a paper bag. The child's voice called again and again; apparently she couldn't tell which part of the huge store her father's replies were coming from. Each time he answered, he seemed to become more irritated with the interruption. Finally, in a fury, he yelled, "I'M OVER HERE!" Glowering with anger and annoyance, he turned to the grocery clerk who was weighing his pears and said, "I'm going to kill that kid, I'm going to tear her limb from limb!"

This was all I needed to hear. He was not only annoyed at being interrupted, but he seemed to have no feeling at all for his child—no sense of how frightening it can be to lose one's parent in a big store. Appointing myself a one-woman committee to protect the young, I began to fume. How terrified she must be, I thought to myself— and all that father is thinking about is his annoyance with his wife for making him go shopping on his day off. I was wavering between going to search for the child myself or telling him what a brute I thought he was, when around the corner of the fruit section appeared a charming little girl about five or six years old. When she saw her father her face lit up with a brilliant smile, and she danced toward him gaily, joining him in his inspection of the apples. I wondered with surprise how she could look so delighted with life when her father was obviously such a mean, unfeeling man. "Can we get some peaches?" she asked. "Dammit, don't complicate my life—there's enough junk on this list. Sometimes I think your mother . . ." Despite his fierce tone and black look, his daughter laughed and said, in an undulgent and loving tone, "Oh, *Daddy!*"

Something was definitely wrong here; there were inconsistencies in this scene that did not seem to have been explained in the child psychology books. I followed father and daughter around the store, listening spellbound as he cursed his way through the shopping list, muttering as he went, "who does your mother think I am? A damn slave? This is a hell of a way to spend Saturday! Come over here Lynn, if you drop one of those bottles I'll break your neck. Get out of the way, you're walking right in front of the basket—all I needed was *you* along to drive me crazy. My God, is there no end to this list? Your mother must think I'm made of money. Lynn, put that back before I brain you. No, you can't have some lollipops and don't ask me for anything else or you'll be sorry."

He seemed so menacing and angry that he scared me, but Lynn was like a gay and friendly puppy, bubbling and bouncing, utterly unconcerned about her father's bad temper. Was she oblivious of it? Children are supposed to feel such things deeply. She didn't seem like an insensitive child—quite the contrary. With her luminous black eyes, lovely warm smile, and easy, graceful way of moving as she skipped happily along the aisles, she was enchanting. The angrier and more caustic the father, the gayer, more bouncy and oblivious to his fury the daughter seemed to be. I decided I had had enough of this confusing and disturbing little drama and went off to finish my own shopping.

By chance I found myself behind Lynn and her father at the checkout counter. He seemed a little calmer. Lynn said, "Daddy, can we get some ice cream cones?" For a moment her father seemed about to explode, but apparently changed his mind. He nodded and said gruffly, "You might as well pick up some lollipops, too." Lynn ran off happily. As she skipped back toward the counter a minute later, she gave her father a look of such love that it was almost too private to watch. He looked down at her, a wry smile suddenly crossing his face, the expression in his eyes suddenly softening. "You're a nut," was all he said, but he reached over and rested his hand on her shining black curls. After a moment he turned away brusquely, busily counting his money.

The clerk smiled at the little girl. "*Kids,*" said her father, in a disdainful, martyred tone. But now I shared Lynn's disbelief and unconcern. That one gesture had told me what I had been too dense to understand before; despite current annoyance, fatigue, and anger at the chores he was performing, despite difficulty in saying the words or showing the feelings, how he *adored* that little girl! And that was what *she* knew about *him.*

The Teen-ager and
the Telephone

The father of a teen-age daughter had gone to Detroit on business and wanted to let his wife at home in New Jersey know he'd be able to get home in time for dinner. First he tried to call from the office he'd been visiting. He tried again at the airport before his plane took off. He tried again at Newark airport, hoping his wife would be able to pick him up. The line remained busy, and after taking a taxi to his home, he discovered his fourteen-year-old daughter still on the phone. "I had been to Detroit and back, all on one phone call!" he said.

The frustration, annoyance—the mounting fury—experienced by this father, is painfully familiar to those of us who live (or try to!) with teen-agers. Any one of us could provide a rich and varied array of "reasons" for that lengthy phone call. Undoubtedly one of the two girls had just gotten a new Beatle record that the other was dying to hear; one of the major functions of the telephone in the adolescent world is to serve as a private radio station playing request numbers! Or there may have been a terrible crisis in school that day; frequently it is the unexpected test announced for the next day's math class—and it should be obvious to anyone that the only way to face such a ghastly event is by talking about it on the phone until time for class!

It is also possible that the Don Juan of the ninth grade failed to say hello when they passed him in the school cafeteria today. In order to fully explore the fine nuances, the deep and significant causes of this social lapse, a full discussion of the matter is absolutely essential before the next cafeteria encounter; this, roughly speaking, may well take an hour and a half. Or there may have been a far more serious crisis on the rocky road to love—a misunderstanding, an argument, hurt feelings—a crisis involving copious tears, long silences, whispered snatches of conversation—barely noted by any attending adult, as the phone is taken into the hall closet for absolute privacy, as the world waits breathlessly to know if all is lost.

Parents find themselves going out of their minds—screaming one minute, trying to reason the next, setting up rules and regulations that are immediately broken, and generally wondering if they will ever again be in touch with the outside world between the hours of 3 and 10 P.M. We joke about it (to keep from crying!); we give grateful thanks for the hours our teen-agers are in school, when, dizzy with rare power, we can phone a friend who's "got one too" and commiserate with each other!

Parents have tried all sorts of arrangements and solutions. Many families have "solved" the telephone problem by letting children have their own phones. This is especially true—and perhaps most easily justified—in homes where constant availability is necessitated by a parent's profession or some other special circumstance. Some families do it simply because they feel they can afford it; some families that could afford it go on struggling with one telephone line, feeling that this is a matter for family cooperation and mutual respect and that more will be lost than gained by "making it too easy." In some homes, where parents tend to feel bombarded by too many people all day, there is a genial acceptance of the teen-ager's long evening conversations; as one father put it, "It's the best wall of defense against being bothered ever invented!"

We all handle it in different ways depending on our feelings, needs, and attitudes. But whatever we do, we often feel bothered and bewildered by it. We might feel more comfortable about living with these adolescents who are attached to a long black wire so much of the time if we had some idea of what it meant to them and why. Why is the telephone apparently an essential life-line? And will this attachment go on forever? While it is true that there are now many adults who like to talk endlessly on the telephone, they are still a relatively small group in comparison with the teen-age talkers. What is it then that makes the telephone so much more meaningful and important to our adolescent children? For all our talk about it, do we have any clues as to why the telephone becomes such a vital factor in teen-age social life? Is it simply that our children have grown up in a world where this is a natural and continual means of communication? Are we parents so old and crotchety that we still view it as a relatively new marvel, while our children take it for granted?

There are undoubtedly many reasons why the telephone is an essential life-line to the teen-ager, but it is my impression that there is a very special reason for its importance—a reason that makes so much sense to me that it has helped me live more tolerantly and optimistically with this phenomenon!

Several months ago I listened to a conversation between two psychotherapists. They were discussing the fact that each of them, completely independently, had discovered that certain of their patients seemed to do much better with "telephone therapy" rather than a person-to-person confrontation. They had both noticed that several patients who had called them at times of great crisis were greatly helped by the ensuing telephone conversation—and never did as well at such moments in the office. In several cases patients had moved away, but contact had been maintained by telephone and the patients often continued to do better than they had done in regular therapy. Having made this observation, they continued to experiment, to talk to other psychotherapists, and they found that this was not unusual or uncommon. It seemed best suited to those patients who were unable to establish intense emotional relationships without great anxiety. They were usually adults of intellectual superiority, but with severe defects in their capacity to deal with the emotional side of life and in relating to other people.

As I listened, it occurred to me that while it might be abnormal for adults to have such severe problems in relating emotionally, it was not at all abnormal during adolescence. This is a period of transition from childhood to adulthood, a time of painful self-awareness, a time for feelings of uneasiness, self-consciousness, a terrible uncertainty about how to behave in relation to one's peers as well as to adults. One has merely to look at their "uniforms"—the long hair over the eyes, the loose and sloppy clothes—to sense that this is a time of life that is filled with so much change, uncertainty, and self-doubt that one wants to hide.

What better way to "hide" and yet be "involved" than by talking on the telephone! As soon as I began to talk to other parents about it, I found that we were all agreed about the fact that our teen-agers were often having more intense and satisfying "relationships" on the phone than they were able to have "in person."

In an earlier age, the first tentative explorations of young people into the realm of adult relationships was probably made via the mails; now the telephone has almost replaced letter-writing, although some parents report that their adolescents seem to write letters to each other in addition to their long telephone conversations. Both kinds of communication offer an opportunity to try one's wings—to practice feelings of love and friendship; they are ways of experimenting with new and often frightening feelings without the impact (and feeling of danger) that may be involved in a direct confrontation. Teen-agers are able to say things to each other that they are not yet able to say easily or comfortably face to face. The telephone permits disembodied voices to communicate with each other without the self-consciousness or shyness of being physically real and present for each other.

Adolescence is a time of life when one must move toward adult relationships involving the strongest and deepest feelings. It is a time of life when young people are exploring their own feelings, finding their own special and individual identities. When one still feels very young and very vulnerable, it is sometimes unbearable and impossible to be close to someone else—to look at them and to be oneself. The thoughts and feelings that one needs and wants to share are too personal, too overwhelming—unless one can share in such a way as to remain physically anonymous.

One mother observed, "From what my daughter tells me, she and her friends discuss some of the most intimate and painful problems with each other on the phone. A father who is out of work, a mother who has had a nervous breakdown, the death of a grandparent, an impending divorce. And yet, when some of these friends come to our house, there seems to be much less serious and private talking. They giggle a lot and study a little—but I have the feeling that their deepest sharing is done on the phone."

When asked about this directly, many teen-agers say that if they want to talk about "something really important" they would rather do it on the phone than in person. This may be due in part at least to the fact that these days our youngsters are precipitated into sophisticated roles too early. They are exposed at the age of eleven or twelve to information, ideas, social relationships, that were once considered more appropriate to eighteen-year-olds. The telephone permits an adolescent who has been catapulted into maturity by today's world to move more slowly, to remain less committed.

In growing up we must all learn techniques and skills for relating to others. When you are still terribly unsure of yourself and don't yet know who you really are, when you are still too self-conscious to ever forget yourself in a genuine feeling of concern for someone else, the telephone can serve as a bridge across an abyss of fear and unreadiness, and through its use, young people practice—prepare themselves for—human relationships as adults.

Youngsters who wouldn't be caught dead reading a book of poetry can read poems to each other on the phone; teen-agers who would die of shame to admit that they still enjoy fantasy and make-believe can play games with each other on the telephone, imagining the future, making up "silly stories." They can share thoughts and feelings that would embarrass them beyond endurance if they had to look at each other!

Several mothers have told me how surprised they are by the number of predatory females that call their twelve- and thirteen-year-old sons on the telephone. This is a good example of what this kind of contact seems to mean to many children—it's so *safe*! Our young teen-agers have been pushed into a kind of social sophistication that was unheard of a generation ago. Whether or not a youngster feels ready for it, he feels compelled to compete, to play the game. Calling boys on the phone is so much easier than talking to them at school! It is a make-believe relationship that does not demand any follow-up, and that is the kind they can handle best. This seems to be the essence of the matter—the fact that relationships don't have to be real, that there is no concrete or final commitment, and that both parties to the conversation can be as sophisticated and self-confident as they feel at the moment, not as they really are.

Our awareness of these factors may help us to be somewhat more tolerant of the disease *telephonitis!* It does not necessarily mean the elimination of all restrictions—that would be unrealistic and not at all helpful in the long run. There is still much to be gained in having to learn ways of living with other people, compromising, respecting their rights. Being given one's own phone in early adolescence, without any restrictions, can be an escape from necessary growth. Even if it is necessary to have more than one telephone line, it is questionable if one line should be the exclusive property of a child; such indulgence may rob him of the opportunity to learn about life and living with others; it encourages the avoidance of those real-life relationships which sooner or later must take over.

The expense is an important factor for consideration; certainly there can be greater leniency when local calls are free. In large cities, parents must help their children accept realistic limits in budgeting phone calls. If teen-agers are old enough to earn money toward their calls, this may be one way to permit them to use the phone more extensively. Parents can acknowledge the emotional needs and the real gratifications that come from these telephone relationships by being willing to compromise—for example, by making most of their own phone calls during the day and asking friends and relatives to call, whenever possible, in the morning or early afternoon. Then if a youngster wants to have a telephone visit of some length, the family can work out a time schedule in which, after a long call, the phone is left clear for at least a half hour afterward so that any important calls can get through. One example of a compromise was that of a family that included—as part of the allowance allotted to their teen-age son—money toward the occasional use of public telephones in order to keep the family phone free. It is also possible that by accepting the usefulness of the telephone to teen-agers parents will be able to get greater cooperation from their children about the matter of polite thank you's and occasional affectionate greetings to grandparents and other relatives and friends. Many parents have discovered that they can avoid a great deal of nagging about the necessity of writing thank-you letters by letting their children phone their thanks, and the results seem to be less stilted, more natural and spontaneous—which makes everybody happier!

Life has changed drastically in the past generation. People talk to each other about subjects that once were never mentioned in polite company—or for that matter, even behind closed doors. Relationships are far more frank and open, and it seems logical that our young people would have to have time to practice, have opportunities to begin relating in this intimate way by "long distance." If, however, they were to go on finding this the most satisfying of all "relationships," we might well become concerned. There are people who have "telephone personalities" even as adults and relate more easily on the phone than they do in person. Our present way of life even encourages this; it is not only possible, but it happens all the time that in our work or daily living we talk to people on the phone, often for years, without ever meeting. Those adults who continually choose this kind of relationship are stunted in their growth; the telephone is not a healthy or mature substitute for person-to-person contacts, even in this automated and mechanized world. Experience in living, the normal processes of maturation, our own continuing interest and concern, will help our children toward the time when real relationships can be as rewarding and safe.

When a youngster says, "I've got to run over to Peggy's house—something wonderful has happened, and I want to see her face when I tell her," or when a teen-ager says on the phone, "Bob, I don't think we should discuss anything this important on the phone, let's wait until study hall tomorrow,"—then we can feel that our children, partly through the opportunity they have had for "disembodied communication," have gained the self-confidence, the sense of personal identity, that permits them to move on to the more genuine and more deeply satisfying contacts of living and loving.

Each year as summertime rolls around I find myself wanting to speak out in favor of goofing-off! It seems to me that today's children, from cradle to college, are spending almost all their waking hours doing something useful, getting ahead, achieving all kinds of self-improvement goals. There is too little time for fun for its own sake and for inner contemplation. One of my favorite people, Christopher Robin, explained it to Pooh this way: "What I like *doing* best is Nothing. It means just going along listening to all the things you can't hear and not bothering."

Unfortunately, it seems more than likely that most of our children will lead a summer life as frenetic, as competitive, as overorganized, as they do all winter. More and more camps are beginning to resemble schools, with special enrichment programs for the high achievers and all kinds of tutorial boosters for the less well endowed. This is often as true for the special programs being developed for our deprived city children as for those privileged youngsters who are heading for expensive camps. It used to be that some of us worried about the emphasis on competitive sports in summer programs; these days we are doing pretty well if children *have* a sports program—they are more likely to be taking advanced science courses in which they are competing frenziedly for prizes for the best science project, or writing poetry or sonatas not for the pleasure it may give them, but in order to do well enough in their work to be chosen for awards.

Let me say at once that I am all for creative pursuits, for stimulating and meaningful experiences that serve to enrich a child's life, make him feel more competent, and give him a sense of mastery over himself and his environment. But it seems to me that we have forgotten the kind of climate in which genuine growth takes place. We are in too much of a rush; we have put too much faith in busy-ness, as if this were the measure of internal progress.

As I talk with parents, many of them tell me that in their school conferences the thing a teacher may be most worried about is that a child day-dreams! True creativity and accomplishment seems very frequently to be related to having time alone with one's thoughts, but we seem to reserve this privilege for adults only.

The pressures on our children during the school year seem to be increasing by geometric progression—and because this is so, it seems to me that one important ingredient we ought to provide during the summer months is time to do nothing. Many parents feel uneasy when a child seems to have nothing to do. They nag when a twelve-year-old sits indoors reading on a sunny day; they get fidgety when a five-year-old spends the morning tossing pebbles into a puddle. What we might well be more concerned about is the child who cannot bear it when left to his own devices, challenged to use his own inner resources. Doing nothing is really doing a lot. It is time to rest, to think one's own thoughts. Just "fooling around" is really a way in which we refill the reservoir of our inner life.

Several years ago, I gathered together some comments of children about what they would like to do during the summer months. One youngster wrote, "I'd like to take a real long hike alone, lasting all summer. At times I might take a boat out on a lake for a couple of days and catch a lot of fish. . . . You would never believe that what I'm really doing this summer is going to a camp with an hour-by-hour schedule." Another child wrote, "My perfect summer vacation would be to live on a desert Island for two months. I would like to have a little house with one door and a fireplace and a television set. The island would have palm trees and monkeys. All day I would play with the monkeys."

It would be foolish and destructive to suggest that summertime could or should be a vacuum—limitless time in which children have no stimulation from the environment, no opportunities to increase their sense of accomplishment. But whether a child goes to a camp or a play group, or whether he travels, he can be provided with some free time, with an opportunity for the necessary pleasures of childhood—private explorations, lazy dreaming, a chance to feel at home in the natural world of sea and sky, sun and grass, insects and animals, whether in a city park playground, at the beach, or at some plush resort.

In the best of summer play programs, provision is made for time with oneself, even in crowded quarters. Rowena Shoemaker, Director of the Play Schools Association, once told me that even when resources may be most limited, as when classrooms in public schools are used for play activities, an attempt is made to find some tiny room, somewhere, that the children call "the quiet room" and where a youngster can take himself when he needs to be alone—where he can look at a book or do a puzzle or just hum to himself, and then return, refreshed. The principal of a school in one of the most deprived areas in the city told me that the best thing he has going for him is a view of the harbor from his office window. He said, "When a child seems tense and unhappy with himself, I invite him into my office and we count the ships going by for a few minutes. It never takes long—after that, we can sit down and talk about his troubles."

There are children who thrive on activity, who want exciting adventures with others most of the time. Certainly we want to provide programs that enhance and enrich, that offer exploration and adventure, but we must also leave room for goofing-off. It isn't a waste of time; it is a necessary interval for refreshing one's soul.

Before we start the frantic rat race about how much a child is learning, what swimming group he advances to, what works of art he produces, whether or not he passes the fire-building test, we ought to remind ourselves that a plateau in development usually results in richer development later on. Sometimes the children who seem to be accomplishing the least during the summer months are the ones who are raring to go and ready for work when summer ends.

Another child, writing about his wishes for summer, put it succinctly when he said, "A perfect summer is doing what you want to do without fighting for it. Think about it! All day, not being bossed by parents, lying on the couch sipping lemonade. Freedom, that's the best!"

I am myself refreshed by the image of this un-bossed creature, supine with his lemonade. At the first opportunity, I plan to take his advice!

Those Blooming Flower Children

[*Author's note*: The following commentary was written for *Newsfront* in the fall of 1968. There was some question about it's appropriateness in this collection because some thought it was dated—that the era of the Flower Children was well past. I feel very strongly that the subject only seems to become more relevant. Names may have changed, but whatever we may call them—Hippies, College Rebels, or Young Radicals— there is a very considerable segment of today's youth who are changing the face of this nation—and, in fact, are representative of a worldwide youth movement. That they are on many occasions impulsive, thoughtless, and impatient for change goes without saying: these are the perogatives of being young. But they are also responsible, I feel, for creating a vigorous new moral force; they are without self-interest and hypocrisy. And I think they offer us the only hope for the world's salvation. That I am not alone in this thought was reassuringly brought home to me at a meeting* of learned government officials, psychiatrists, psychologists, and sociologists dealing with the problems of arms control. There was a general concensus that the human race simply had to find an alternative to power as a source of security; that weapons of war have become so destructive that no country could safely attack an enemy without also destroying itself. "What we need to do," I heard them say, "is take a lesson from the young people who descended 400,000 strong on Woodstock† and, despite the discomforts and

* American Psychological Association Annual Convention, Sept., 1969
† Woodstock, N.Y., Music Festival, Summer, 1969

hardships of creating an instant-city, without adequate food or sanitation and three days of rain, lived together without violence. The new secret weapon they seem to be suggesting as a substitute for power is *caring*."]

If you want to make a middle-aged parent really "blow his cool," all you have to do is take him to the East Village for an afternoon, or to Sheep Meadow in Central Park on a balmy summer day. There you can watch him go mad over the beads, bangles, and beards, for whether personally involved as the parent of one of this new breed, or merely a spectator, the over-forties are not happy about those blooming flower children!

For the last few years, as one of those involved, I've tried hard to keep young by being open-minded—somewhere or other I read that open-mindedness is a better youth preserver than hormones—but I must admit I've had my ups and downs. There are moments when it all repels me completely, and other moments—and these have been increasing in number and becoming more compelling all the time—when I am deeply moved and greatly heartened by our flower children.

I am *not* speaking here of the sick; in every generation there are bound to be a small percentage of young people—fragile, anguished, in deep psychological pain—who express their inner problems through taking on the very worst characteristics of the particular milieu of their own times. There is nothing new about this, the wounded-in-soul are always among us. I am speaking of that large segment of our youth whom *we* see as being shook-up—those who seem to be in rebellion against middle-class smugness, hypocritical platitudes, and the terrible reluctance among us ancients to accept change. Among this large and diverse group are many sub-species, but there are some generalizations that apply to most of them.

I am not a historian, but I would wager a guess that never before in recorded human history has the younger generation been so concerned, so committed, so active, in the social issues of the times as this one. In a society as disease-ridden as ours, caught in the grip of the most vicious race prejudice, it is our *young* who understand what must be done in this land. There is among them a poignant and shimmering compassion for each other that

totally disregards color. They are also the first generation
of young people who see the impossibility of settling
problems by war, they cannot be made blindly nationalistic by the waving of flags or the sound of marching bands,
but they take their stand as members of the human
family, without concern for national boundaries.

Next time you find yourself despairing over the younger
generation with their annoying refusal to accept our way
of running things, I invite you to join me in a painful but
very enlightening game that I have been playing. The
name of the game is, What Are They Telling Us and How
Did They Get That Way? Why the flamboyant disregard
for proper attire? Why the emphasis on loving relationships without concern for social regulations? Why the lack
of any consideration for the external appearances of
things, which we interpret as laziness and sloppiness? Why
do they give things away so blithely, share their money so
unconcernedly? Why do they take over college buildings
and jeopardize their chances for a diploma, almost
achieved? Why do they work in Bedford-Stuyvesant and
Watts for a pittance, and then storm the doors of the Dow
Chemical Company, an organization only too eager to pay
them well and retire them early on gorgeous pension
plans? Why do they burn draft cards, and go to prison, or
to Canada? Anybody who is willing to really investigate
the consequences of these acts knows very well that this is
no fun and games, but a terrible and painful facing up to
about as much agony as most of us have experienced in
forty or more years of living. Why are they dropping out
of school—and *into* life?

The answer—if we are honest about it—is shocking to
a tired parent's nervous system. The answer, my friends, is
that *we wanted them this way*! If you think you can take
it, let's look back together to the early 1950's when we
were the young and eager parents of this generation of
teen-agers. What sorts of things did we begin to tell our
children when they were four or five or six? I know what
I was saying—that war is terrible and that we had to find
some better way to solve international problems; that
people are the same all over the world—that there were
good people and bad people in China, in Russia, and in
the United States; and that most people want to live in
peace and love. That it was a shame on our history and

national honor that we treated Negroes and Indians, Mexican-Americans and Orientals, like second-class citizens and that our only salvation was a genuine belief in the brotherhood of man. That one shouldn't judge a person by how he looks or what he is wearing, but what he *is*, inside: that is, not to trust externals, but to be concerned with how a person lives his life with other people.

Weren't a great many of us saying that material possessions are unimportant, that what *is* important is the sacredness of life? Weren't we saying, don't judge a man by his credentials—his diploma, his insurance policies, the number of cars in his garage—judge him by what he does for other people? It seems to me that many of us were appalled in the 1950's by what Harold Taylor, (then president of Sarah Lawrence College) called "The Understood Generation"—the young people of college age who seemed totally indifferent to the social stresses of McCarthyism and the Cold War and simply wanted that $40,000 house in the suburbs and the best investment plan for early retirement. We despaired over the conformist youth of that time, and we exhorted *our* children *not* to do likewise. "Get in there and *care!*" we said to them!

Now we look at the crazy costumes and the sandaled feet, and the fury at poverty and hate, and the refusal to be interested in neatness and order and getting one's union card for economic security—and we shudder. Can these be *our* children? The trouble was, we weren't listening to ourselves. We were busy making money, getting comfortable, putting up with things as they are. But our children *did* listen, and I for one am proud of them.

SECTION
III

Seeing Yourself
in Your Child

We were having a conference at the nursery school, and the mother sitting opposite me was saying, "Tracy is stubborn and strong-willed and one of these days I may kill her." Then she added, not at all to my surprise, "Of course she's just like me."

Over and over again this theme seems to be repeated— the great oversensitivity to likenesses between parent and child. One probable reason for this is that very few people seem to grow up really liking themselves. It seems to be the nature of things that what our parents found difficult to handle about us, we came to view as handicaps, when in truth, these may have been some of our more important qualities. It is hard to handle a noisy, obstreperous kid with a mind of his own; it is hard to raise a child who desperately wants to be independent. It is nerve-wracking to have a child who is so curious and daring and adventurous that he gets himself into one scrape after another. And as any parent can tell you, it is harder to raise a creative, sensitive child than a placid, stolid type. And yet all these deplored qualities may become the sources of unique strength in adulthood. However, by that time, we have usually accepted our parents' distress as a judgment, and self-contempt, self-hatred, are common feelings.

Then, when one's child turns out to have the same tendencies, we are really in a bind. How can we bear to let a child have the same qualities that bug us about ourselves? We identify our child's characteristics with our discomfort and unhappiness as children, and every indication of similarity between us is salt in a raw wound.

That's one kind of overidentification with children that may make their growing more difficult. Another kind is where we cannot endure their frustrations and pain. *They* may have the strength and toughness to endure those ordinary stresses that are part of living and growing, but we cannot bear it because we are overinvolved. The mother who recalls the agonies of being a wallflower at her first dance falls apart when her teen-age daughter isn't asked to the school prom by the boy of her choice; a quiet, introverted father finds it unendurable when his son can't fight back when he's picked on by the school bully. Our children, who may have none of our anguish about these issues, are surviving quite well—are nowhere nearly as upset as we are—but old wounds make us more susceptible and twice as vulnerable.

Of course there are rough and difficult times when children need our help and compassion to surmount some stumbling block to growing up—but that help is likely to be far more meaningful if it does not include inappropriate over-personalized empathy.

Another overidentification hang-up is when we need our children to live out our dreams—where, in one way or another, there has not been enough fulfillment in our own lives. A sense of emptiness makes us revel in their good grades; a lack of focus in our lives makes us dream of some professional success for a child who as yet hasn't a thought in his nicely normal head other than the next baseball game; we curdle at his penmanship at nine—how can he ever be that judge or senator we dream of? When a parent's life is barren and unfulfilled, each triumph seems to be his instead of his child's. Such overidentification with a child's successes can interfere with his right to his own growing as much as identifying with his setbacks and failures. Whenever you succeed at something just to please a parent rather than yourself, a kind of impurity comes into the struggle.

Loving and letting go doesn't start in adolescence. It really starts at two and three, when parents must make the first step in letting a child become *himself*, with no strings attached. A child cannot carry the burden of old hurts, unfulfilled dreams, feelings of inadequacy, remembered wounds—the freight of our adult memories of child-hood. He wants and needs to be seen as a totally new human creature who will have every opportunity to see his life in his own way and who will mold himself and his experience originally and uniquely.

It is one of the most difficult tasks of parenthood—but perhaps the most rewarding—when a parent can give the supreme gift of allowing his child to be himself, to experiment with his likenesses and differences from his parents and everyone else, unimpeded in his search for his own identity by the identity problems of anyone else.

Guilty Parents
and How They Grow

It almost never fails—each time a new mother comes into my office at the nursery school, she starts the confer-ence off by saying, "I suppose now you'll tell me all the things I'm doing wrong." What a brainwashed lot we are, we parents! It wasn't always thus.

A few years ago, I was meeting with a group of mothers in a discussion series that took place in the home of one of the group members. During one session, her mother, who was visiting, listened in on the discussion. Grandma was obviously fascinated and horrified as she sat listening to the worries and anxieties of the younger gen-eration of mothers. She kept shaking her head in wonder and sympathy, especially during a discussion of how a mother could get her housework done, take the children out to play, and also have some time to rest herself. After the meeting she came up to speak to me and told me that she'd enjoyed the meeting, but she couldn't understand why young mothers worried so much. "You all act like you need a college education to raise children. How do you think we did it? People have been raising children for thousands of years without worrying every minute," she assured me. Then she said she would give me an example of how she used to relax when she got tired as a young mother. She had eight children and she lived in a tenement on the Lower East Side. On the first balmy spring day, she would line her children up, two by two, and march them several miles to Central Park. There she would find a sunny hill, and she would lie down on the grass, instructing her eight children to sit in a circle around her. She would tell the children that this was a special park for mothers to rest in, but that there were kidnappers who steal mothers there. She said they must sit and guard her while she took a nap. Then, shrugging her shoulders, to show me how simple life could be if you just had good sense, she added, "They got the air and I got my rest."

I have never forgotten that charming lady or her advice because it was such a perfect example of the difference in our generations. Can you imagine how guilty a parent would feel about doing something like that today? The trauma it might cause a little psyche to hear about mother-kidnappers! Why, we would assume that our children would be scarred for life!

A young father once told me that he viewed the changing patterns of child-raising practices in terms of white-meat chicken. He explained that when he was a child, his father was very much the head of the house. When the family sat down to Sunday dinner, Father stood at the head of the table and carved the chicken. Mother was served first, father, second, and then each child from oldest to youngest. This young father had been the youngest of five, and since he was served last, he had last choice. As a result, throughout his childhood, he had never tasted a piece of white meat, and he daydreamed about the time when he would be the father and would have second choice. "Now I'm a grown-up and a father," he complained to me, "and I *still* don't get the white meat—the children get first choice!"

A mother once wrote and asked if I knew any cure for child psychology! I am not too sure just what she had in mind, but I suspect a good beginning might be made if we judged ourselves less harshly and demanded more from our children. We have demanded superhuman wisdom and patience from ourselves, and have tended to be too permissive and undemanding in our dealings with our children. We have a right to rest and to eat white-meat chicken too, if we want it, and our children are not little hothouse plants; they need and can accept limitations.

A French mother, after asking about the nature of my work, said very sadly that there was very little child psychology in France. "All we can do," she said apologetically, "is raise our children by the heart." I have never been able to forget that conversation, because I found myself feeling that I was more to be pitied than she. It is time we learned to combine our useful new information with a little careful listening to the heart.

On Blowing One's Top

A mother told me recently that when she objected to her son's yelling at her, he replied, "If I can't get mad at home, where *can* I?" It seems to me a reasonable question. We all have to blow our tops once in awhile, and a strong and resilient family seems to be just about the best safety valve we've got going for us.

One mother told me about a therapeutic blow-up at her house. Her two sons Andy and Pete, aged seven and nine, had been home from school with one flu bug after another for about three weeks, and to make it even worse, once they were convalescing, the weather was too bad for them to go outside. Everybody was getting on everybody else's nerves. "When I woke up in the morning," this mother told me, "I'd wonder what scene from a Tennessee Williams play was going to be enacted in my living room that day. I felt terribly cowardly because I didn't have the guts to kill myself."

That morning Andy and Pete started picking on each other the moment they woke up, and by noon their fighting had reached such a crescendo that Mama was shaking. She told me, "Between the yelling, and the running noses and the dirty pajamas and the chaos in their room, I was ready to give them away—as if anyone would take them!" She realized she was on the verge of a nervous breakdown, so she tried to pull herself together. She said, "I decided to try to be a good mother if it killed me." Taking a deep breath, she suggested in her most dulcet tones that they have a tea party—a really fancy one. The boys were delighted; she got out the good china, the linen table mats, the hand-embroidered napkins. They made decorations for the table, and then they made some cookies and cocoa. As life returned to some semblance of tranquility, she began to think, Maybe there is something to this psychology business. Just as she put the cocoa on the table, with a can of Redi-Whip, the telephone rang, proving that there are no happy endings in real life! Being an experienced mother, she told the boys not to touch the Redi-Whip until she came back and she made the conversation just as short as she possibly could; but by the time she returned, the boys had taken the Redi-Whip and squirted it directly into the cocoa, managing to get cocoa on the table mats, the upholstered chairs, and the beige rug. She told me, "You know, for a minute I sort of blacked-out—and then I just went berserk. It was the last straw and I guess a screw came loose. I took that can of Redi-Whip and I squirted it on the kids, chasing them all around the apartment, getting whipped cream on the walls and everywhere—just running around like a crazy nut, yelling and squirting. Suddenly I came to—My God, what was I doing? What a way for a mother to behave!—I figured I must have scared them to death. Then I see they are rolling around on the living room floor, absolutely hysterical with laughter—they're just dying, they're laughing so hard! We had a marvelous time cleaning up—we laughed all afternoon and got hysterical all over again telling my husband about it that night—and now, every time I get to the end of my rope and I yell "Redi-Whip," they know it's time to shape up—or duck. Do you think I scarred them for life?" she asked me.

Quite the contrary; it was just the clean breeze blowing through that household of boredom and restlessness and itchy-ness that everyone needed. It was a hilarious lesson in human frailty. Ever since I first heard that story at a PTA meeting many years ago, I've wished I could have been at that tea party!

We can't yell at the boss or the teacher or the butcher or the cleaning man; we try to be sweet and polite to our neighbors and in-laws; *something's* got to give once in awhile. Maybe we have underestimated one of the most important attributes of family life—that home is the only place in the world where, when you really let your hair down, they don't throw you out. In fact, sometimes they even like you more, afterward! There's nothing in this world to match it.

Humor Helps

One of the most important aids to living reasonably with children is collecting phrases that make you laugh! I think this is one of the most sadly neglected areas of parent education. It is a game in which each family has to accumulate its own special phrases, but I have found that a great many of them can be shared by all of us, since most of the crises in family living are pretty common stuff.

Let's face it—there are things about living with children that try the souls of any grown-up, no matter how patient and mature. For example, there is that interminable period of growth when a child becomes totally incapable of seeing what is right in front of him. I recall one such day, when my daughter was about seven, when in fifteen minutes of "looking" she was unable to find the red sock that was lying on her white pillow, two feet from where she was screaming that I'd stolen it. Later that day, when I mentioned the morning's beginning to a sympathetic friend, she responded, "Oh sure, I know exactly what you mean—I call that *'thing blindness.'* "

If all of us are afflicted with a disease, it seems to me it helps a lot if it has a name. I have never again been as bothered by that miserable routine of "Where is it?" "You're not really looking." "Yes, I am," since I have known its name—thing blindness. What such phrases do is put things into perspective through humor, and somehow it helps to clear the air.

A father told me that when things get rough at his house, they call it a "socks-in-the-soup kind of day." "With five nutty kids underfoot," he said, "there are days when I get laryngitis from yelling, and my wife's frayed nerves just seem to be dangling all over the place. On one such day, when the two older boys were carrying on a running battle about something or other, and Kathy was crying in her room over some boy who'd hurt her feelings, and the baby was teething, and Kenny broke the washing machine, we all sat down for supper so mad at each other, and so fed up with family life, I didn't see how we could get through the meal. Helen slammed a bowl of pea soup down in front of me, and as I started to eat it, in stony silence, I discovered the baby's sock coming up on my soup spoon. The resulting hilarity cleared the air—and now when any of us say "I've had a socks-in-the-soup day,' everybody knows it's time to get out of the way."

A mother told me that the one thing that always drove her husband out of his mind was when the children kept asking *why* when he'd set the law down about something. Having been a major in the army, he suddenly hit on the perfect solution for those occasions when he'd had it up to here with democracy in the family. One question too many and he would stand at military attention and announce crisply, "It's policy." That was the sign to his children—if you ask why once more, you will be in more trouble than you can handle. It works—even for less military types—because it has just enough of a gleam of humor in it to help everybody shape up without prolonging the agony.

Another source of misery for many tense and tired parents is what goes on at the dinner table—the kicking, the jumping, the shouting, the fighting, the sleeves used as napkins, the belching contests—it is often more than a sensitive adult can endure. On one such occasion, when the container of milk was knocked over and the splatter was greeted by uncontrollable giggles, Father rose in his wrath and shouted, "OK, that's IT—now CIVILIZE UP." I recommend the effectiveness of this command when one has reached the end of one's rope. It is succinct, and everybody gets the message.

In another normal household, when two of the four kids had had the measles and were slightly stir-crazy, and number three fell out of a tree and was bawling so loud that mother lost her cool and spilled some grease which set the oven on fire, father leaped for the fire extinguisher, shouting "All hands to the misenpoop!"—at which point everybody rose to the occasion like sailors in a typhoon, cleaned up the mess, and calmed down. Somewhere in America, at this very moment, there is a family who are ready for that command, that nonsensical but effective message that the moment of truth has arrived!

In our house, we discovered that anything that sounds like German has a special air of authority and can be employed very effectively when parents have reached the end of reason and patience. Especially at bedtime—after the fifth request for a glass of water, the continuing patter of tiny feet, the giggling that goes on after the last and final command "Go to sleep." At this point, my husband, summoning to mind all the wartime movies about Nazis, would shout "Aus, Aus, bei mit zeit von zu—Zu bet Gehagen Haben ist" or sounds to that effect, and that was *it* for that night. Why did it work? I think because it combined both desperation and humor—and that seems to be an excellent combination for those times when all else fails.

In all fairness, one must add that there are times when *children* need a phrase or two to turn *us* off, when *we* are being pests. The one I like best and that I here bequeath to the younger generation arose out of a nine-year-old's desperation when, while happily lolling in his bath, his mother kept up an annoying stream of instructions about washing behind his ears and between his toes until he muttered, "I could love you so, if you'd only shut up."

What lies behind all such moments in family life is laughter—a wry awareness of the funny side of our sometimes too serious efforts to live together in love and harmony. They remind us of our clay feet, our human imperfection; they bring the laugh that relaxes—for, as one bright youngster put it most succinctly, "If you can't be a silly jerk sometimes in your own family, where *can* you be?"

Working Mothers

Several years ago, I recall seeing a cartoon which showed a somewhat pompous and fatuous-looking man sitting on the living room couch telling a guest, "No wife of *mine* is going to work!" In the background of the picture one could see through the doorway of the kitchen what appeared to be an overburdened, harrassed, downtrodden lady, surrounded by five or six kids, dirty laundry, a sinkful of dishes, a large pot overflowing on the stove, and other equally compelling indications of pure chaos.

With that picture in mind, before talking about *career* mothers, let me state categorically that *all* mothers are *working* mothers. Homemaking is an honorable and challenging profession that can use every bit of talent, imagination, patience, and intelligence a woman can bring to it—and if a woman wants to make that vocation the central force in her life, she should be free to do so without Betty Friedan and her girl-militants breathing down her neck and making her feel guilty because she isn't out there running for President.

At the same time, there are many of us who need a broader range in which to fulfill ourselves—and the load of guilt we carry about child- and husband-neglect is utterly absurd. A case in point: a mother who came to see us at the nursery school—ashamed, apologetic, flooded with guilt, eager to tell us that she would give up her job if we felt she should, because four-year-old Andy was having nightmares and she was sure he was showing his resentment and anxiety about her working. She was just about ready to turn in her attaché case when we pointed out to her that about 70 percent of a nursery school population have some nightmares, a symptom almost invariably cured by getting to be five or six years old. Andy was a cheerful, self-reliant, charming little boy, and maybe he *did* get mad sometimes when his mother wasn't at his beck and call, but he had an adoring father, a baby-sitter who worshiped the ground he walked on—and a mother who arrived home from the job she loved, two hours after his return from nursery school where he was having a perfectly fine time, thank you. We career mommas have been horribly brainwashed. It is my impression that our children get too little neglect! We hover over them like anxious idiots, fearful that the fact that we are fulfilling ourselves must somehow mean we are depriving them. Nothing could be farther from the truth. The more any human being lives out the best that is in him, the more he respects and enjoys the full range of his own talents and creativity, the more he can infect others with his joy in being alive and his sense of wonder at what human beings can do.

The mothers who tend to read the most stories to their children, who play house until the thought of another tiny cup of tea can send them screaming, who play the most games of Candy Land and Monopoly when their kids are sick, are career mothers! Why? Because we are afraid we are depriving our children, and we do penance for the pleasure we have in being completely ourselves. The mother who feels she is available all the time has no guilt, so even if she has spent the whole day cooking or cleaning or mowing the lawn or reading a good book—not exactly devoting all her time to her child—when Junior comes and asks for a game or a story, she is less likely to snap to attention.

It is partly our heritage of Puritanism, I suppose; if we are enjoying our lives, we get scared! It is also the helpful hand of J. Edgar Hoover and assorted judges who have blamed juvenile delinquency on working mothers, managing to overlook the voluminous evidence that this has nothing directly to do with the matter. It is also that hard core, right-of-center group of psychoanalysts who go on telling us that our psyches really cry for total submission to dominating males, and that despite Woman's Suffrage and modern technology, we would be much happier still boiling the clothes on the stove, cooking oatmeal overnight, and spinning our own wool.

Having two careers certainly isn't for everybody. You

do have to be a little crazy! There are days when you want to kill yourself. You *do* need a very special kind of husband who is willing to sacrifice his peace of mind in order to stay married to someone who needs to test herself in more ways than most. When a virus hits the whole family and your careful schedule goes to hell on a bicycle, or when you miss the school bazaar and your daughter looks wistful even though two Grandmas and Daddy were there, or when you come home half-dead with fatigue and realize you forgot to defrost the lamb chops—then you think you ought to have your head examined.

But on the whole, we do both jobs well; if we didn't, we wouldn't try so hard. It is wonderful to be in love with life—to love our families, to know they supply us with a central core of meaning, but that it is also wonderful to live in a time when we can also explore our own souls, sharpen our talents, study and discover, search for what is best and strongest in ourselves. When a woman is thus fulfilled, she is a constant reminder to her children that finding one's own special life and being is the most important task, for in doing that, in caring for your own life, you become a person who can care deeply for others.

Telling It
Like It Is

In spite of the enormous changes that have taken place in our understanding of what makes people tick, I still detect a certain tendency to try to raise children by the Pollyanna Glad Books. For those of you who are under forty, this was the title of a series of books about a young lady who devoted her life to trying to see the bright side of things. As I look back on my generation's youthful devotion to her, it seems surprising that more of us didn't go into diabetic coma from all that sweetness!

I was reminded of this approach to life a few weeks ago

when we were at the beach with a young couple and their two-and-a-half-year-old daughter. Jenny did what every two-year-old does the first time at the seashore—there was all that lovely, cool water, so she plunged into it with mad abandon and got the shock of her life when she lost her balance. Daddy raced to the rescue, and as Jenny blubbered and choked and howled, he kept saying, "That's all right honey, there's nothing to cry about—you're just fine." Jenny yelled louder and it occurred to me that her reaction was perfectly appropriate—everything *wasn't* fine at all—the water had betrayed her completely, leaving her with watery sinuses and hurt feelings. Did it really make her feel better to be told she was fine? Somehow I don't think so. She might have recovered her equilibrium faster if Daddy had said, "Poor Jenny, you got scared, didn't you?"

How often have we said "It doesn't hurt" when it *does*; "It's not scary" when it *is*; "You shouldn't get angry" when the child *is* angry; "There's nothing to be shy about" when a child is *feeling* shy? It's an understandable delusion we try to defend; we don't want our children to be afraid or angry or shy or in pain, so we fall back on a somewhat primitive and childlike way of neutralizing reality. But it isn't especially helpful to our children. My experience has been that a child is much more likely to be able to bring his resources of strength and endurance to an unpleasant or difficult situation if we acknowledge that that is exactly what it is. If we say to a screaming youngster, "The doctor isn't going to hurt you, so stop crying," he is likely to yell louder because he feels quite alone with his misery— undefended and misunderstood. If instead a parent says, "I know you're scared, it's all right to cry—hold my hand and it will be over soon," chances are better than good that the child will feel so strengthened by this moral support and the recognition of *his* reality that he will muster all his courage and become a quietly gulping stoic.

When our daughter was about five and had to have some stitches in a bad cut on her hand, the nurse said, "Don't cry now, you're too big for that," whereupon our wiser pediatrician responded, "Don't say that—she's a *little* girl, and it's all right if she cries." Later the doctor told me that when she was a medical student and she had told her first young patient not to cry, he had vomited on her instead! She said, "I learned the hard way that nature's way is best—tears have a purpose and there's no reason to deprive a child of the best way there is to express fear."

A twelve-year-old has a math test coming up and is terrified. Does it help to say, "You have nothing to worry about"? Or might we relieve some of the anxiety more effectively by saying, "Sure you're scared—you and every other kid who ever took a math test. It's a natural thing to be scared at such times, but you've done your work and that's all you can do." A fifteen-year-old doesn't want to come in to greet our dinner guests—he says he's too shy. Chances are no one will get a look at him if our answer is, "What's there to be shy about? They're old friends—they've known you since you were a baby. Don't be silly." Maybe if we said instead, "I know you're shy—it's a stage—so just come in with a tray of hors d'oeuvres, like you're helping me, say hello, and leave." The trouble with *that* system, I ought to warn parenthetically, is that it is so reassuring that you can sometimes find that fifteen-year-old sitting around talking to the guests twenty minutes after you're wishing he'd go back to his own room!

We are myth-makers too often. We say things like "She's a *lovely* teacher," when we know perfectly well she's rotten; or "There's nothing to it," when we know that learning to ride a horse isn't exactly a breeze for everyone; or "There's nothing to get so angry about," when a youngster's sister breaks a favorite doll—even if it *was* accidental, we know perfectly well it can matter terribly.

There is something to be said for the notion "The truth shall make us free." Saying it like it is, can be a source of encouragement and help to a child, while playing games with reality can only make him feel defenseless and alone. One can endure almost any frustration, any discomfort, any anxiety, if it is acknowledged by others and can be shared. There will be a far greater capacity for making the best of it if a parent says, "You're right, she's a teacher with a bad temper. I know she makes you nervous—I wish it was different, but since that's the way it is, let's see how we can make it easier for both of you." Or, "Yes, some people find it very scary to get on a horse for the first time—it's so high up, and you don't know what the horse is going to do—but if you can stand the fear for a little while, most kids love it. Let's see—if you're still scared after a couple of tries, we'll put it off for awhile." That is a likelier road to equestrian joy. And there's nothing wrong with acknowledging that one feels angry when someone breaks a favorite toy—that is a sound and appropriate feeling, and accepting it doesn't mean that you are allowing a child license to express that anger in ways that are unacceptable. Maybe, instead, it will just clear the air. One of the most compassionate and constructive results of our increasing understanding of human psychology has been our ability to understand and accept all kinds of feelings.

What a lift it gives to the spirit to know that one's human feelings are perceived and understood by others! It's enough to make cowards strong, blushing violets the life of the party, and an angry foe a friendly ally.

No Hiding Place
Down Here

Helping children to understand and accept real feelings is fine; but we often come dangerously close to overdoing a good thing when, in an effort to be understanding and insightful, we walk around with an analyst's couch on our back, analyzing and interpreting every mood, every experience. Children have a right to privacy in their feelings too. We have seemed, sometimes, to come to the conclusion that the verbalization of insights is always a good idea—that the more we analyze our children's feelings the more they will be able to cope with them. This is simply not true.

For example, there was a great and good lady-psychologist in the 1940's by the name of Dorothy Baruch. Based on the best information of that era, when "insight" had become a kind of catechism for what was at that time the more rigid orthodoxy of psychoanalysis, she recommended that whenever possible, parents help children to understand the unconscious motivation behind their behavior. If Betty knocked over the best lamp in the living room, Mama was encouraged to say, "That's all right, darling—I guess you broke the lamp because you really wanted to hit the baby. You're angry because he's been getting so much attention." This approach to child raising—through insight into unconscious motivation—had some great and good things in it. It was compassionate and nonjudgmental; it was kinder than parents had ever before been encouraged to be. But it went too far. We have discovered since then that insight isn't enough; just understanding why you do a thing does *not* necessarily neutralize the behavior—we humans seem to be much more complicated than that. The field of psychotherapy has gone far beyond those early stages, and we know that understanding a problem is only one dimension of its solution—sometimes a very small part of it. Insight wasn't enough because it cut off experiencing life deeply and naturally. Some things in life ought to be *felt*, not explored and analyzed. Some things ought not to be talked about—not because they are bad or sinful, but because in talking about them feelings become too antiseptic; one loses a necessary depth to one's inner life.

The other problems in emphasizing insight in child raising, were 1) that our interpretations could sure as hell be wrong, and 2) that the theme song of our children's lives could become "No Hiding Place Down Here." Even the most experienced psychotherapist makes many a mighty error in interpretation; one hopes that he is skillful, wise, and humble enough to question his judgments and that his patients are hopefully autonomous enough to say "No, you're wrong about that." Children are least likely to think their parents are wrong—so they are stuck with misinterpretations. Secondly—and this may be what drove so many therapist's children to other therapist's offices—children had no *privacy;* there was the constant feeling that *nothing* was ever sacred, nothing truly belonged to oneself—no emotion could be genuinely experienced, everything became grist for the clinical mill. I recall one psychiatrist who reported that his daughter, in exasperation, once said to him, "Don't tell me why I did it—just punish me and let's get it over with!"

In recent years I have lived with the happy delusion that we were making real progress in using the best of our earlier learnings in psychiatry and psychology—balancing this with later information. For example, we were realizing that it could be beneficial to help people understand human motivation, but that in the normal run of parent-child relations this might be done most effectively by generalizing, rather than by making a child feel he was living under a microscope. It was quite appropriate to say to an older child, "When a new baby comes, older kids can get pretty fed up with all the attention they get—that's a natural feeling." That's a potentially helpful generalization because it offers solace for ruffled feelings but leaves room for the child to make the choice of seeing a connection with his own feelings, or not.

Another thing we seemed to be learning was that it was possible to respond to a child's feelings, when he made them perfectly clear, with sympathy, but without taking away his right to experience the feeling. One could say "I guess you're pretty sore at me for breaking my promise" without analyzing the omnipotent parental image of childhood, or one could say "If you're feeling scared, we'll leave the night light on" without explaining that phobias may be the result of unexpressed hostility! Compassion and understanding are helpful—constant analytic vigilance is not. Some problems are necessary—and privacy is sometimes more important between parent and child than understanding too much. A psychologist friend told me that when his ten-year-old son told him of a dream in which Daddy went around the house with a jeweler's magnifying glass in his eye, he knew it was time to keep his practice of psychotherapy at the office for paying customers only!

I thought we'd made all this progress, and then along came Dr. Haim Ginott and his best-selling book and the language of "childrenese." Here we were again, being encouraged to interpret every feeling—but with greater impact this time around, because while Dr. Baruch left it up to the parents to choose their own words, Dr. Ginott provided lesson plans in home-therapy, telling parents what words to use—and even what voice to say them in. And once again, the issue gets murky, because no one in his right mind would suggest that it isn't a grand idea to be kind to kids, and to try to understand them, and to help them to understand themselves to some degree.

The danger lies in becoming therapists instead of parents, in creating a clinical relationship instead of a spontaneous and unselfconscious one through which one can experience genuine emotions. What scares me is that insight may become programmed, sterilizing our feelings.

It is a difficult line to walk—trying to be aware of a child's feelings, but not interpreting so much that the child is robbed of his right to what is irrational, creative, and passionate in his nature by use of a surgical probe. It's a difficult balance to achieve, but it offers more hope for salvation than becoming insightful robots.

Are We Afraid of Our Children?

We were at a dinner party and a few of us were half-seriously bemoaning our fate in being the parents of teen-agers: how to endure the certain knowledge that if next month's phone bill exceeds the last, AT&T will announce a further stock split; the fears that flow uneasily through one's mind when Junior doesn't seem to be doing any homework for days on end and those college boards are looming; the embarrassment when a wild apparition in flowing cape and torn blue jeans sails through the living room where Dad is offering his boss a first cocktail; the discomfort of long black silences that may last for days; the terror that strikes when that "baby," so carefully nurtured on Gerber's best and gallons of cod liver oil, tells one that marijuana should be legalized because if it isn't, 85 percent of his friends are breaking the law.

"Everything we've mentioned are things that we don't like," one father observed, "and it's gotten so that everytime we get together, we bitch about it all—but we don't do anything about it."

"That's true," a mother replied, "Honestly, I think I

spent the first half of my life being afraid of my parents, and now I'm spending the second half afraid of my children!"

How could this have happened? How could our feelings toward our own youngsters have come to differ so radically from the way that our parents and grandparents felt about their children? It seems to me that part of the answer to this question is the enormous impact of the psychological revolution that has taken place since Sigmund Freud's voice began to be heard. In its simplest terms, today's parents feel culpable—they feel that everything they say and do to their children will have a lasting effect for good or evil. We have been taught to think in terms of psychological cause and effect; we have been made acutely aware of the complexities in the emotional relationship of parent and child, and we have become—too many of us—the first generation of uneasy, embarrassed, inarticulate, and immobilized parents.

As part of the same picture, we have come to want our children's love more than anything else; it represents proof, in some confused and distorted way, that we are doing a good job. It was far easier for our less psychologically sophisticated ancestors to discipline their children, since their central goal was respect. We are afraid even to be disliked, and out and out fury, even if momentary, seems unendurable. We have tended, in seeking the worthy goal of a democratic family life, to forget that adults still must retain authority and power and that an inevitable by-product must be a certain amount of hatred!

In addition to being overwhelmed and therefore frequently paralyzed by our new knowledge about child psychology, we also live in a time of such rapid social change that we find ourselves feeling estranged and alienated from our children as they approach adulthood. The generation gap grows wider by geometric progression as the world our children know and seem to understand appears more and more confusing to us. We are afraid of doing or saying something that will be psychologically unsound, and we also feel that we can say and do nothing because we don't understand our children and the world they inhabit. We are not only afraid to enforce rules and regulations— we are afraid to *make* any because they might be wrong! But even if we thought we were right—how tough do we dare to be? We are also afraid of the autonomy of young people—our child might take off in a huff and join an LSD club in some hippie neighborhood, labeling us as failures forever. If we sit tight and keep our mouths shut, provide room service, a generous unearned income, free cars and guitar lessons, and a wayside hostel for friends and casual acquaintances, who knows, we might be able to get our child into college without his noticing!

Of course I'm exaggerating—but I hope with a purpose. If it is at all true that we are afraid of our children—and I think the evidence is considerable that we are—then obviously it must be having some serious consequences for our children. It may well be that some of the characteristics they manifest most strongly and which we dislike and fear the most, may by a curious kind of irony be related specifically to having a set of fearful parents!

There is nothing wrong with humility; a healthy self-questioning is of course a civilized and mature approach to life—if it doesn't go overboard. Today's watchful parent who is afraid to hurt his child's psyche by saying or doing the "wrong" thing is a far more sensitive and well-informed human being than the stern, frightening, authoritarian parents of another age, ready to charge in with terror as their major weapon for child raising. The problem is to find new alternatives—some healthy balance between red-blooded self-righteousness which permits you to do just as you please because you are sure you are right, and too great passivity which comes with an awareness of one's human frailty and limited understanding. It is wise and responsible to learn as much as one can from all the helpful new insights available to us, but we cannot afford to be immobilized. Children need parents as much as they ever did—parents who can take action, who will be protective, who will give guidance, even when they are not entirely sure of every step they take. This was expressed with succinct clarity by a sixteen-year-old pregnant girl who, when her parents faced this serious crisis with strength and forcefulness, said, "Do I have to get into real trouble before you let me know what you think is right or wrong?"

New knowledge never imposes impossible standards on us—*we* do that ourselves. Perhaps our new understandings about human personality are still too new to wear with comfort, like stiff shoes that make one walk with caution. We are beginning to realize anew that one must *act* in life without having absolute truths to back us up.

No matter how rapid the changes or different the world, our children still must have some guidelines, even if they are slightly old-fashioned and dated! And even if they must eventually be rebelled against. Growing is a kind of exploration for which you need *some* kind of map of where you are heading; then you can modify and change it as you go along, learning from experience, testing yourself in relation to the terrain—the unforeseeable demands and challenges.

Fear produces a vicious cycle in parent-child relations. When we become afraid to follow our feelings and instincts or to say what we feel and what we think is right no matter how loudly our progeny may howl, we create anxiety among our children who, although they would probably deny it indignantly, feel that something is very much missing in their lives. One way to fill the void is with things, and we begin to find ourselves being asked for material gratifications that we feel uneasily are inappropriate. Because we are behaving unnaturally and do not feel free to express our love as much through demands and limits as through giving and giving-in, we don't feel free to withhold what our children really do not need, so we give them things they ought to be making or earning themselves in order to gain a sense of personal accomplishment and pride. The relationship slowly deteriorates into parents giving and children taking with less and less engagement between human beings who matter to each other and need to be communicating about much more important matters than how much allowance is not enough or too much. As one mother put it, "I just don't understand what's the matter with me—I would really like to know what Ken is thinking about, I'd like to really talk to him, but I never seem to be able to overcome some inner hesitancy. So I end up yelling about the clothes on the floor and we're more out of touch than ever."

Our children are frequently good teachers; most of us have been brought back sharply from our hesitancy and fear to the reality of the fact that our children still need us very much by what they tell us through their behavior. A father of my acquaintance told me that he had become more and more uncomfortable in the presence of his fifteen-year-old daughter's friends, who all seemed to him to be rude hooligans. They would ring the doorbell, walk in past him with a grunt, sprawl on his furniture, raid his refrigerator like a horde of locusts, leave his books and records on the floor and the record player running, and then depart with his daughter, vaguely muttering something about a demonstration at city hall. Slowly he began to realize that he was letting these young people behave in a way that was absolutely guaranteed to make him feel nothing but outrage and loathing, and he began to wonder why he was afraid to act like a parent. Deciding he was on a murder course, he gritted his teeth for a major policy shift. When the next long-haired young man in a tattered civil war uniform mumbled his way past the door, Old Dad said, "Look here, I've decided that in my house I expect to know the names of the guests and I expect them to say hello and shake hands. If you're visiting my daughter, I expect you to show some respect for my belongings and to put them away before you leave." This young man, caught as number-one guinea pig in this new experiment, couldn't have been more surprised or pleased! He smiled affably, gave his name, shook hands, and said, "I'm really glad to meet you. I like your taste in music."

This father has been gratified to discover that his daughter seems to like him a whole lot better now that he has remembered his role as a civilizing influence, and in addition, he has found that he has opened up an opportunity to talk to young people. He finds them exceedingly interesting, and struggling very hard to come to terms with the complexities of modern living. He told me, "I really respect these kids. They dress weirdly, and I don't understand a good thirty percent of their idiomatic speech, but they are full of real insights and feeling. They don't scare me anymore at all!"

The only way to relate to children at any age is to insist on having a relationship; you communicate by communicating, by saying what you think and feel and doing what seems right in a given situation. Within the framework of participation and action, one also has the necessary right and obligation to backtrack, start over, change and make amends, which can't be done at all when one remains isolated and passive.

One of the current difficulties besetting many parents and children is that they feel shy with each other; at the same time that parents are scared to make a wrong move, their children are hampered by an accentuated shyness and clumsiness in adult-youth relations. The formal, ritualized social manners of the past are gone; in many ways this is a good thing too, in the sense that they were often hypocritical. But they didn't last so many hundreds of years without being useful; for young people, who were taught the social amenities early in life, knowing how to say "How do you do," when to stand and when to sit, how to express gratitude, thoughtfulness, and respect, were really convenient crutches while one was young and unsure of oneself. Because we do not train our children in these techniques, we have to help them learn other more direct, open, and honest ways to communicate with adults. We have to take the initiative and in effect say, "I want to try to understand how you feel; here's how I feel. We aren't going to succeed in this altogether, of course, but I want to keep in touch with you."

There are some ways in which I think a little fear of our children may do us a world of good. I sometimes wonder whether I'd be a very good citizen if it wasn't for my fear of losing my teen-age daughter's respect! During a teachers' strike in New York she heard me holding forth in righteous indignation against it—that there was no moral justification whatsoever for making children the pawns, the innocent victims of a power struggle. This was during a very busy time when I had several writing assignments past due and a number of speaking engagements to prepare for. She caught me up sharp one day, saying, "If you feel that strongly about it, why don't you volunteer to teach—you have the background and there's a school right across the street. If you can't bear to watch the deprived children of New York suffer any more deprivation, well, put your money where your mouth is!" I was "afraid" of her because she was absolutely right! And I went—and discovered how little I knew about meeting the needs of today's city children and how desperately they need our attention and concern. It was a rough few days, and I wondered often if I would have stuck it out without her challenge.

Our young people care deeply that life should have

significance, and it is possible to become allies and friends when we make it clear that we respect the values that they feel are important. One mother who had silently and inactively opposed the war in Vietnam was finally challenged to take part in a protest march when her son told her she ought to "put up or shut up." She told me that this event had had a marked effect on their relationship. She said, "You know, I still feel sort of uneasy when I lay down the law and insist that Dave has to be in by a certain time on school nights, and that cold, disdainful look I get still makes me shrivel up inside, but somehow all the talks we've had lately about the war and civil rights has made me feel we really respect each other and I can stand the anger better."

There have been a great many learned articles written about the hippies, and one of these attempted to document the ways in which parents were responsible for their children becoming hippies. The nineteen-year-old son of a friend of mine read the article, and when his mother asked his opinion of it, he said, "I can't get over the *arrogance* of parents who dare to think that they are responsible for everything we have become! We are individuals in our own right—I wish you'd all give us credit for making *some* choices for ourselves, with our eyes wide open." It must be very demoralizing for our children to be witness to our feeling so responsible for everything they do. It makes them seem like puppets we manipulate on a string, with no autonomy, no freedom to make their own decisions. If parents and their children can shake free of this weight of culpability, they will all be free to respond with more genuine spontaneity to each other—asserting themselves without fear, testing their strengths, sharing in a genuine encounter, with all the clashes as well as the moments of empathy that any real relationship creates.

A friend told me that one day she was walking on a deserted beach often frequented by teen-agers. She saw, scrawled in the sand, "PARENTS DO NOT EXIST." How sad it would be if all young people were to feel our fearful abdication from authority was that real; it is surely a time to take courage and be ourselves. It's the best way to help someone younger do likewise!

The Generation Gap

It seems to be generally assumed that the generation gap is the result of adults and teen-agers not understanding each other, of living in different worlds. I have begun to have some doubts about this interpretation. It seems to me that the generation gap disappears almost completely when parents start acting like grown-ups and that the gap widens in direct proportion to the idiotic ways in which adults are trying to be exactly like their children.

How many dinner parties have you been to lately where serious, hard-working, intelligent middle-aged people have sat for almost the entire evening tensely straining to try to catch the mumbled, muffled words on some folk-rock record that is supposed to have some deep and mystical meaning? Have you been to a suburban cocktail party lately? You know who's wearing the beads and the beards? You know who's boasting of trying pot? The papas who catch the 7:20 A.M. commuter, that's who! And how about all those middle-aged ladies with the fat knees, scantily clad in microskirts and getting chillblains all last winter? It seems to me the widest gap in the generations is occurring in those places where parents are making the biggest fools of themselves, pretending they are kids.

Many parents, afflicted with the Youth Cult of our times and desperately trying to reconnect themselves with their adolescent youngsters, seem to have become involved in a frenzied attempt to take on all the characteristics of youthful rebellion. No matter what outlandish lengths our young people may go to achieve a distinct and separate look, we are never very far behind. A good example of this is the wildly energetic music and dancing through which teen-agers have tried to develop a style all their own. Who's dancing to the wilder tunes? Well, the discotheques are crowded with the Teeny-Bopper Serutan

Set—to the delight and profit of the orthopedists, who will be able to retire on substantial annuities because of the middle-aged enthusiasts busily snapping their sacroiliacs in wild gyrations that are unbecoming and inappropriate to their (you should pardon the expression) age level. A TV commercial tells us, as we watch three pretty young things having fun at a carnival shooting gallery, "One of these teen-agers is really a thirty-year-old housewife." The implication, loud and clear, is that this is the goal we have set for ourselves—to be indistinguishable from the young. For some strange reason, we have concluded that all we have to do to bridge the generation gap is to become slightly ridiculous imitators of the young. That may be what is driving our kids away.

There is clear evidence that this is so, for in the past several years, as some parents have started acting like grown-ups, one sees the gap almost disappearing. I first noticed this myself in April of 1967. Up to that time, most of us had left the burden of examining the moral and social issues of the war in Vietnam up to our young people; the point at which a great many of us decided that maybe grown-up parents ought to be concerned about this issue was the first nationwide Peace March—and as my husband and I took that first step back into responsible citizenship, I realized that for the first time in many years I felt close to young people, and they were letting me back into their lives. There was no generation gap in that march—despite an age range from infancy to those in their seventies and eighties. There was no generation gap at all in the New Hampshire presidential primary in 1968. Politics aside, and whatever the ultimate consequences, at that time Eugene McCarthy acted like a grown-up parent, concerned about the serious problems besetting our land. Instead of trying to be a crazy kid, he acted like a concerned father—worried about the state of the world in which his children, all children, were living. Thousands of our supposedly irresponsible, thoughtless, lazy, self-centered kids cut their hair, donned clean shirts and knee-length skirts, and went to work.

Dr. Spock isn't alienated from young people—perhaps he's the best symbol of all of a parent who brought himself back into the historical role parents have fulfilled in the past: the moral leader who can be respected and admired. It wasn't enough, he discovered, in the early 1960's, to instruct mothers in how to make formulas—a grown-up parent also had to concern himself with whether or not there was Strontium 90 in the milk. Wherever and whenever a grown-up parent has taken up the fight for what he believes, commits himself to the profound and challenging issues that face us, the generations close ranks.

In the past, parents maintained their role of moral leadership without concern for the generation gap. I suspect that this is why the gap was narrower—not simply because life changed more slowly than it does today.

Every generation of young people has found it necessary to rebel against the older generation, to flex its muscles and indulge in some emancipation acrobatics as a way of establishing itself as the coming new order. This process is essential to human growth and social change. But the widening of this gap seems to me to represent far more than that rapid rate of change. There is a deeper alienation—today's young people just plain don't like us very much, they don't admire us. They think we are flighty. self-indulgent hypocrites and frauds. We talk a good line about integration at our segregated cocktail parties; we are for peace, of course, but Junior mustn't jeopardize his Harvard scholarship by demonstrating; we are shocked by four-letter words appearing in hippie publications—when these words don't even begin to describe the sexual shenanigans of the wife-swapping set or the conventions of middle-aged dirty old men in any of the fancier hotel chains. Instead of serving as models. instead of behaving like responsible and concerned adults willing to commit ourselves to some genuine goals and ideals, our children watch us—in pity if we're lucky, in rage if we're not—as some of us make asses of ourselves pretending we are sixteen again.

Our children do not relish this social palship we offer them. They would prefer to keep their clothes, their music, their hair styles, for themselves. What they want from us is social parenting—this couldn't be any clearer than it is as they rally with love around the parent who climbs back up on the ramparts where he has always belonged. The gap disappears when a *grown-up* appears on the scene.

The Care and Feeding
of Parents

For approximately fifty years the United States has been developing the art of parent education. Succeeding better than they dared to dream, experts—from the maternity ward nurse to the college guidance counselor (to say nothing of the nursery school teacher, the grade school principal, pediatricians, psychotherapists, social workers, anthropologists, sociologists, FBI Directors and irrascible old judges in between)—have managed to destroy forever that curse of earlier times: the self-assured, secure parent. Clarence Day of *Life with Father* fame remains a curious relic of an unknown species to the blithering idiot parent of today.

While a certain amount of self-doubt is good for the soul, and even for the raising of the young, it seems to many parents and experts alike that perhaps the pendulum has swung too far; in concentrating so much of our attention on potential traumas to children, we have neglected the delicate and difficult ages and stages in the life of each parent. Now that our children have the righteous self-confidence that we once possesed, it seems only fair to turn the tables once again. It is time for *parent* study by *child* educators—a program to teach children the problems and pitfalls of parenthood so that they may try to do a more sensitive and constructive job in nurturing their parents from twenty to fifty years of age. One can only hope that after a period of publications and lectures we might come full circle and find that children are, again, afraid of parents.

There are many areas in which parental insecurity is a serious matter and where the mental health of parents seems to be moving rapidly in the direction of greater instability and breakdown. Take for example the situation in which a modern parent is confronted by a request from

a child and realizes that finally he has been asked for
something he *really* cannot afford to give; he managed the
car and the sailboat, and was grateful for more minor
demands for Bongo drums and a summer vacation in
Katmandu, but he realizes with a shocking jolt that if he
buys that island in the Bahamas he will have to go into
bankruptcy. It would be helpful, in line with a new approach to parents, if Anna Freud, for example, would
write a book for children entitled *The Real and the
Fantasied Guilts of Forty-year-olds*. In addition to covering
situations such as the above, involving panic-reactions to
not being able to give adequately, such a book might
cover the problem of more intangible giving as well. For
example, there is the problem of the parent who is forced
to face the fact that love is not enough. Neither was
private school, three psychoanalysts, a progressive sleep-
away camp, understanding, companionship, and acceptance; his kid is still a bum. This is known as the Where-
Did-I-Fail? syndrome. It is based on a faulty and primitive
perception, endorsed in the early years by some experts,
that good parenting could produce instant success. This,
perhaps more than any other delusional system, is now
causing some of the most severe identity crises among
parents—especially between the ages of thirty-five and
forty-five.

Because parents have become so sensitized to their
responsibilities, the changing moods of their children tend
to show another side of their increasing instability. It
would be helpful if someone with real stature, genuinely
admired by young people—like Bob Dylan—would point
out that the tendency of teen-agers to fall in and out of
love with so many threats of dying is unsettling to parental nervous systems, so easily threatened by thoughts of
desertion.

Actually, this matter of desertion is probably one of the
most crucial and important subjects in relation to parental
care and feeding. We might ask Dr. Spock to write a book
entitled *Separation Anxiety in Child-Parent Relations*.
Here he might discuss the tremendous emotional crisis in
the life of a parent the day his child *willingly* goes off to
nursery school, or says that the second-grade teacher is
smarter than Daddy, or prefers to eat supper at a high
school friend's house every night of the week because

"Sandy's parents are really cool." There are literally thousands of serious separation traumas for parents, and they have not been given the proper attention or concern during these years of focusing on child development.

A parent who has been led to believe that he is the center of his child's universe may show a serious setback in his growth and development if he does not get homesick letters from his child in camp. A parent who has prided himself on being a loving confidante may suffer severe ego-disruption when he realizes that when he walks into a room occupied by his teen-age son or daughter and their friends all conversation stops dead; for months or maybe even years, one may see a hurt and bewildered look in the eyes of such a parent—who also finds constant confirmation of his feelings of rejection and unworthiness in locked desk drawers and locked diaries: salt in the wounds of his palship vision of parenthood. One of the most heartrending separation traumas that I can recall hearing about was the pre-menopausal mother, already suffering from feelings of inadequacy, who arranged with great difficulty to sleep in the hospital room of her ten-year-old son so that there would be no serious emotional disturbance following his appendectomy only to hear him say, "Ma, I want to go in that big room down the hall where all the kids are. You can go home." A shock of this kind may cause permanent damage to parental self-esteem.

During the early years of mothering and fathering, parents are given some unconditional love and genuine acceptance by their children; there *are* some warm and happy moments when children make their parents feel wanted and loved. However, these decrease more rapidly than we have been properly aware of, in our concern with child-growth.

Fortunately—if this were not true, few parents would reach old age with any semblance of mental health—separation traumas come gradually, increasing in intensity, allowing some time for adaptation and acceptance. First Father, sweating and panting profusely, begins to get a vague sensation that he's not wanted at Little League try-outs; Mother is told she is not to attend the PTA-sponsored Halloween dance at school because her dresses are too long, her hair too short, and her voice just a shade too loud. The degree to which parents are able to adjust to these early signs of rejection will depend of course on their early childhood experiences and the inherent degree of flexibility in their personalities.

But no matter how subtly and gently separation experiences may gradually increase, observation seems to indicate that the problem of family outings remains a source of great disturbance to many parents, no matter how strong their healthy strivings may be. It is necessary for children to come to a greater understanding of the role they play in helping parents to cope successfully with the gradual decrease in togetherness. One set of parents who had planned a midwinter vacation in Florida and had offered to let their thirteen-year-old daughter bring a friend along were devastated when her response was "Ugh! What a horrible idea! I don't want to go anywhere with *you*!" This unfeeling child caused her parents to go into a state of passive depression during the entire Christmas vacation.

Another family reacted more aggressively, with open hostility. Plans had been made for an Easter-week visit to Williamsburg, and although there was, to say the least, a large absence of enthusiasm on the part of their three children, aged seventeen, fifteen, and twelve, the parents, with grim determination coupled with the small vestige of authoritarianism left over from their grandparents, launched the trip. Once the experts begin to really guide children more successfully, the ensuing disaster will become less commonplace. It rained for a week and the car broke down three times. The seventeen-year-old went for long solitary walks and caught cold. The fifteen-year-old rented a bike and only appeared at the hotel at dinner time. The twelve-year-old watched every TV program from 8 A.M. to midnight for five days. Shaken to their roots, these parents had to face too suddenly and too quickly the terrifying thought that after all these years they might be alone together again. Children could be most helpful in preparing parents for this eventual reality if they tried to make the adjustment palatable for their parents by slow stages. For example, in the case above, the children might have said, "Gee, we'd just love to take a trip with you, but we all want to keep up with our schoolwork during the vacation—why don't we just spend one wonderful day together and go to a movie and have dinner out?" While intelligent and sensitive parents may begin to smell a rat under such circumstances, there is at least the saving of their pride and the substitute reward of conscientiousness on the part of their children.

There are ways in which separation is made somewhat more palatable by outsiders. Just at the point where parents of teen-agers are convinced that they are morons, social pariahs, and hardly worthy of life at all, some young person comes to visit one's child and actually resists being shoved immediately into a candlelit room. He or she, for a moment or two, while one's child is off-guard, actually seems to be enjoying a parent's company. It is fleeting—and no child worth his salt will permit it to get out of hand—but it may encourage a parent to look with some hope toward the future; one cannot hope for acceptance from one's own child, but perhaps a future daughter or son-in-law will find one lovable.

In the end, as in all things, personality differences will out. The parent who has tended all along to be particularly dependent on his children for love and security and who is unable to adjust successfully to new situations suffers the most and needs the most help. There is the story of the forty-seven-year-old woman who was crying bitterly and copiously after the wedding of her youngest child. "My life is *over*," she sobbed, as she emptied ashtrays and folded chairs. "All my children are gone—what is to become of me?" Her husband, the product of late weaning and self-demand feeding, therefore with greater inner resources for self-acceptance, suggested quietly, "You might try getting married."

As opposed to this sad example of maladaption on the part of a mother, there is the story of the cop who found a couple necking in a car on the grounds of a college. Flashing a light into their startled faces, he was informed, "Officer, we have just delivered our youngest child to this college, and this is the first time we have been alone in eighteen years!" With broadminded compassion, the policeman retreated.

There are beginning to be other hopeful signs. In one family where the children tried conscientiously to prepare their parents for their departure—where, indeed, they had explained with great sensitivity and understanding that parents must learn to love and let go—Mother and Father found themselves alone in an empty and quiet house. They walked from room to room—affectionately patting an old teddy bear, picking up an array of clothes on the floor, closing a closet door on old beer cans and hockey sticks—and finally, sitting down on the living room couch, tenderly holding hands, looked each other in the eye and said, "Alone at last—isn't it *great*?" Slowly but surely we must find ways to encourage and reinforce this kind of healthy maturation. We must arouse in our youngsters a sense of responsibility, a genuine concern for the difficult and painful aspects of parental growth and change; we must enlist their guidance and help in the worm's turning.

No Shortcuts
to Growing

Wherever you turn these days, someone is trying to make children grow up faster and more efficiently than nature seemed to intend. Five-year-olds are having facts yelled at them in "Follow-Through" government-sponsored programs, babies up at Harvard are being programmed to perform all sorts of intellectual gymnastics between burpings, and mothers of infants are being given conversational scripts to perk up any drowsy-headed toddler. After all, there is no time to be wasted! These intellectually stimulated babies will probably have a life expectancy pretty close to a hundred years—and it is certainly a matter of vital concern whether they read for ninety-seven years or only ninety-five.

At the same time that this mass insanity is going on with young children, thousands of damaged adults are in the process of trying to heal the emotional wounds of a lifetime through the processes of psychotherapy. And a major factor in this undertaking is the painful necessity for somehow finishing the unfinished business of childhood. The adult who was forced to be brave too soon faces his cowardly feelings and relives them; the person who was never permitted to mourn the loss of a parent grieves agonizingly on the therapist's couch; that eldest child who had to take care of six younger brothers and sisters faces his need to be irresponsible, dependent, help-less, and cared for. The adult suffering the tortures of intestinal spasms deals with the toilet training that came too early and too severely; the obsessively hungry, greedy adult begins to recall infantile feelings of starvation from being forced to adapt to that four-hour feeding schedule.

If we have learned any one thing in all the years of investigating the human psyche, it is simply this; if a child skips any normal and natural phase of his development—if he is pushed or pulled too fast, if nature is not given time to help him grow—he remains forever twisted and deprived, unable to fully measure up to the capacities that may be in him until, through psychotherapy or life experiences, he is enabled to fill in whatever unmet needs and unfinished feelings there may be lying beneath the surface of his experience.

In fact, this phenomenon has been so well demonstrated by clinical psychologists and psychiatrists that in some cases real regression has been found to be a useful antidote to later difficulties. In psychotherapy the patient may experience old unfinished business in thought and feeling only. But in some research projects, direct regression has been used very effectively. For example, one imaginative project involved allowing emotionally starved children raised in institutions to regress to babyhood in a life situation that allowed them to become babies again. Each child was permitted to be as much of a baby as he wanted to be. He could sleep in a crib, talk baby-talk, wet his pants, be rocked to sleep in a rocking chair by a nurse, and so on. It was discovered that children who were allowed periods of such regression were able to make far better adjustments to later foster placements than another group of children who were taken from orphan asylums and placed directly in foster homes. That is only one example of many similar experiments which have confirmed the observations of most psychotherapists that you just can't get much of any place at all if you're feeling bad about old miseries—about pieces that were left out in your growing up.

In spite of incontrovertible evidence on this matter, we find ourselves inundated with programs for early intellectual stimulation and acceleration, doing everything possible to circumvent the natural events of babyhood, refusing to enjoy the wonders of infancy or let our babies be babies. There is every reason to believe, in the light of what we know, that these unnatural infants who are being taught to read and count and reason and anticipate—figure out all the dumb puzzles we invent for them—may well be a generation who, as adults, will appear to be feebleminded. We will have to invent new kinds of regression for them, permitting them to babble and suck and crawl and cuddle and gurgle before they will be able to pick up their lives and become thinking adults—curious, resourceful, and intellectually alert.

This further evidence that human beings seem to have a remarkable capacity for learning nothing whatever from experience is especially unsettling to those of us who were unfortunate enough to be born at a time when it was fashionable to use conditioning techniques for controlling our digestive tracts. That was the era when mothers were being urged to leave nothing to nature's imagination; we were "programmed" by six months for habits of eating and eliminating—and many of us have the digestive disorders to remind us of this era. It makes us wonder—even despair—at the thought of what sort of intellectual disorders will evolve from today's conditioning of the mental functions of infancy.

SECTION
IV

Getting into the Nursery School
of Your Choice

It was bad enough when parents and their teen-age children were having hysterics over the problem of getting into college; it is too much to bear when one begins to see the same kind of anxiety and carrying-on associated with getting a child into the nursery school of your choice!

The situation in New York City is somewhat exaggerated (we have a talent for always getting into bigger trouble here), but it is symptomatic of a mood that seems to be permeating our society in general—and that is the unexamined assumption that the more time a child spends either in school or studying, the better off he will be. Please notice that I said "studying"—I didn't say "learning." Learning goes on all the time—especially when it is not interfered with too much by educators!

Getting into a so-called "good" nursery school in the New York area now involves filling out application forms that sometimes rival in length those required by colleges. In most cases applicants must appear for an examination. This may mean that the child is watched by a team of experts while he plays; often it means he will be probed by a psychologist while his parents get the once-over from teachers, social workers, nurses, and graduate students working on theses. One parent, crushed by a school's rejection of what she considered to be her brilliant, charming, and talented four-year-old, asked for an explanation and was ready to measure out the hemlock when she was told, "Our tests indicate he does not have college potential." Imagine! At four! To have one's whole future read in the cards! And what stupid cards they are! There

147

is absolutely no correlation between aptitude or I.Q. tests during the preschool period and later academic success or failure.

Yet I have seen strong men weep and otherwise moral and upright women offer large bribes when children have not made the grade into that marvelous nursery school that feeds its population into that absolutely necessary private school that feeds into only the best prep schools and Ivy League colleges. In case you haven't followed this particular madness of the 1960's, the importance of getting into the right nursery school rests on the fact that if you make the wrong move there, your child is forever lost to second-class citizenship!

If it wasn't funny, it would be obscene. As a matter of fact it *is* obscene. It is part of the general panic about getting children smartened up. We figure we have failed to solve any of the serious human problems that beset us as a nation, so, in looking for simple answers to this awful dilemma, we have latched onto the notion that being smart will fix things up. It won't. Being kind and compassionate and sensitive and honest would help much more, but it is too hard to provide an education that teaches those virtues. It is easier to stuff a lot of irrelevant facts into our children's heads, so we decide to start teaching reading at two or three and to get those kids into school as quickly as possible.

Is nursery school important for children? It can be a lovely, magical time for a child who is curious, adventurous, eager to play with others. It can be a time of wonderful growth in a school that is concerned with *children* and how nature provides for their growth, rather than with what they will do when it's time for college. It can be an excellent way for mother and child to begin to separate and for both to acknowledge their own special needs and interests. But it all depends. If you've only been alive for *thirty-six* months, maybe you still have some unfinished business of being dependent in a properly babyish way. Some children need more time to grow alone, time to grow in their feelings, time to be mothered some more—and if they do, that is no sign of hopeless depravity. It used to be, when there was time for childhood, that baby stayed by mother's knee till six or seven. And there are some pretty rotten nursery schools that push and pull and try to turn out a regiment of mechanical dolls who all look and act and learn alike—and any child would be better off at home than in a school that has no respect for differences in growing and for the sanctity of each child's right to be himself. Nursery school ought to be a pleasure— a first step out into a wonderful world of joy and excitement in learning, in discovering love and warmth in strangers, in taking the first halting steps in the process of becoming a civilized human being; it ought to be a place to learn about oneself and others, to explore the world in one's own special way and at one's own pace.

But there are many ways in which such pleasures can be obtained in a young child's life, and if he doesn't want to go, or if you can't get him in, chances are he will survive. While history doesn't provide any scientific proof, as far as we know, Socrates, Shakespeare, and even our own George Washington never went to nursery school.

A Proposal To Teach Reading
in the Third Grade

There is probably no educational controversy that rages more wildly than the question of when children ought to be taught to read. At one extreme are the people who say we are wasting valuable time if we let our kids just lie around, growing—that we ought to start teaching reading at ten months or even earlier. Some of the more conservative members of this group suggest waiting until two, when one can proceed to teach typing at the same time. I suppose if things go on the crazy way they've been going, someone will find a way to beat nature's timetable and accelerate finger coordination, so that one won't have to wait around to begin typing school. Sooner or later I expect someone to come along with an intrauterine teaching machine.

At the other extreme are the experts who tell us that all sorts of terrible things can happen if we start reading too early. There is research that suggests that if a child tries to begin to coordinate his eyes in order to recognize letters and words before his eye muscles can really handle this (sometimes as late as six or seven), he may well become a one-eyed reader. Neurologists tell us that there is such variation in neurological development that there may be an age span of two or more years in the physiological maturity of first-graders. Educators report that an individual child may show as much as a three- or four-year age span in different kinds of maturation—that a seven-year-old may have the mental ability of a nine-year-old, the social sophistication of a four-year-old, and the physical coordination of a six-year-old. These variations in growth rates mean that some children may be ready for reading in kindergarten while others may not be ready until second grade or later. A recent investigation of the Gesell Institute reported their conclusion that 50 percent of the children now entering first grade are not mature enough to achieve what is expected of them.

I am inclined to agree with this judgment—but not because *children* have changed in any way. Today's fives are just as bright and perky as they've ever been, but they are up against a society which has decided that it knows better than Mother Nature how fast they ought to grow up—a society that has fallen madly in love with computers and would like its children to become more like them.

It would be nice not to have to become partisan about the two extreme points of view. It would be nice to live in a world where each child was deemed to be a new discovery—an uncharted sea, where no one tried to impose external rules and regulations, but where we watched the *child,* instead, and while providing him with a loving and stimulating environment let him tell *us* when he was ready. But such good sense seems quite remote, and during this period when the pushers are in the ascendancy, I have decided to take a position about as far at one end of the scale as I can get.

I propose that no child be *permitted* to learn to read until third grade—that teachers in kindergarten to second grade be instructed to thwart any evidence of a child's disobeying this rule, In this way, every kid who is ready to read, somewhere between three and seven, will have to learn on the sly, by himself. He'll have to sneak books under the covers and learn by flashlight. When he goes to the public library, he'll have to stand on tiptoe and lie about his age, making reading just about the most exciting pastime ever invented. The advantage to all this is that teaching *oneself* to read is far superior to being taught. This should be perfectly obvious because children teach themselves to speak with almost no failures. Have you ever heard of a child flunking talking? The percentage is negligible compared to school records on teaching reading, where failures sometimes outnumber successes.

Furthermore, those children who are not ready to read until seven or eight would not become second-class citizens. Under my plan a child could even get to be eight years old without feeling that he is a hopeless moron who will never learn anything. It is possible that without having to worry about learning to read, most children will develop remarkable and outstanding talents that would never have emerged if they were struggling with letters. Under my proposal, by the time a child got around to reading, he might already have become an amateur astronomer, a happy ornithologist, a singer or poet—or so enthusiastic about all there is to learn that he will be a successful schoolboy before he can even spell cat. His teachers would be on their toes, too, having to keep up with a wide and exciting assortment of interests while reading to children. Having had several years for running and jumping, such children will probably be ready for sitting still, too.

There he is now—shiny and bright-eyed and eight years old—shall his teacher teach him to read? Not on your life. Teachers have been too corrupted by reading theories; they tend to be fanatics of one kind or another, some believing in the religion of phonetics, others seduced by one or another of the overpriced systems planned for them by psychologists who have had very little contact with children. The ones to teach the third-graders ought to be the sixth-graders—and not necessarily the best readers. There is a good deal of evidence to suggest that the best reading teachers are children having trouble learning to read themselves—they can pick up the trouble spots faster! They also tend to be quite compassionate, and there can be one teacher for every student—an excellent arrangement.

I predict that if my system were to be adopted, there would soon be an underground movement dealing in contraband books and that our children would manage to outwit us—learning to read in their own good time, but ready for anything by third grade.

A Message from
an Underachiever

A college professor of my acquaintance recently began asking his students how they viewed themselves during all their school years from nursery on up. He discovered that eight out of ten of the students in his classes had always viewed themselves as underachievers—as never having lived up to teacher's or parent's expectations. It would seem that within the past ten or fifteen years of rapidly increasing mass insanity about education we have managed to burden almost all our children with a sense of current or impending failure, which we, as adults, do not share with them at all, having grown up, perhaps, in less hysterical and demanding times.

God help any of us over twenty one if we were to be judged for underachievement the way our children are today. I can't recall any time in the last twenty five years when I have spent four hours of any evening memorizing facts that bored the hell out of me. When I want to know something that I haven't the background to understand, I go and find someone who is an expert and he explains it to me: I don't take a three-credit course in a subject I may never need to know anything about again. I feel perfectly free, at the end of a hard day's work, to goof-off: to gossip with a friend over a drink or to watch some real trash on TV. No one could get me to devote my time to studying subjects that I know I would hate to my dying day and could never do well at no matter how I tried. It is a glorious thing to be a grown-up and to have my achievement level left entirely up to me. As a matter of fact, it is just because it *is* left up to me that I work pretty hard at what matters to me.

The label of "underachievement" is never really a measure of a *child's* success or failure; it is really the way in which educators avoid taking responsibility for evaluating the educational programs they offer children. If a child is bored or scared or unmotivated or unchallenged, we say he is an underachiever. That takes the onus off us to find out why he is any or all of those things.

All human beings are underachievers—if by that we mean that we never fulfill all the possibilities within ourselves. All human beings ought certainly to be helped in every way possible to make use of their gifts in ways that bring a deep sense of joy and well-being. But that kind of achievement bears no relation whatsoever to what is meant on most report cards. It is not that the child is not achieving meaningful goals for himself, but that his teacher really doesn't even *know* what his goals are, and is merely speaking of the level of achievement she requires.

When children are called underachievers, what we ought to understand is that this represents the failure of the teacher and of the system to stimulate, entice, free a child's own instinct for growing and learning. It is also simply a measure of the fact that a child, in the game of pleasing others rather than oneself, isn't usually willing to do more than any adult would do.

There is no way of measuring the full potential of any human being—we can only assess little bits and pieces, and with the clumsiest tools. What we ought to be doing is concentrating all our efforts on finding better ways to help children do their own assessing, by providing an environment so full of possibilities, so warm and supportive, so rich in learning experiences, that each child will find himself involved in a personal struggle *with himself* to learn more, to feel more, to live more fully, without competing with anyone else—each human being encouraged from birth to find the self he needs and wants to be. That is the only kind of achievement that matters to us as adults. Why must we deprive our children of this inner quest for selfhood by blocking their path with the narrow, rigid, limited goals that lead them to *meaningless* achievement—which seems to me to be a far greater crime against life than underachievement.

Testing

One welcomes whatever comedy relief one can find about schools these days, and I was grateful to a teacher who provided me with some. She teaches in an East Harlem school in New York which had been in a state of seige for months, after a very long teacher's strike—the students evidently feeling they were giving back as good as they got from adults. One day she saw the school psychologist flying down the hall after a student, shrieking, "He stole all my intelligence tests!"

Now there's a student with real creative potential! It takes wit and wisdom to see the obscene irrelevance of a testing program in a school that is going up in smoke, and in which anyone with half a brain can easily see what deprivations exist, as well as what is needed to change the climate of these students' lives; the kind of love and patient understanding, the therapeutic teaching they need, we aren't prepared to give them—and a testing program is no satisfactory substitute.

The issue of school testing is bigger than the current crisis. John Holt, author of two beautiful books, *How Children Fail** and *How Children Learn*,† ·said recently, "Almost all educators feel that testing is a necessary part of education ... I disagree—I do not think testing is necessary or useful or even excusable. At best testing does more harm than good; at worst it hinders, distorts, and corrupts the learning process." I'm with him one hundred percent. If testing had anything to do with genuine growth, we would go on giving tests to people all their lives. We don't, because we know perfectly well that whether one matures or not depends on things that are not measurable in adulthood. It's only children for whom we have a separate philosophy.

Some tests are necessary, of course. If you want to be a

* New York: Pitman Publishing Corp., 1964.
† *Ibid.*, 1967.

violinist with the Philharmonic Orchestra, you have to show what you can do; if you want to improve your typing, you give yourself time tests. But virtually none of the testing done in schools is of this kind, the kind in which one is tested to prove one can perform activities one has chosen for oneself. We say we give tests to see what children have learned, in order to help them learn more. Mostly, that's a damnable lie. We test in order to threaten children into doing what we want them to do, and in order to set up a basis for handing out punishments and rewards suited to the competitive nature of our educational system. Why should the learning process be competitive at any time in one's life?

Churchill once said that the teachers at Harrow were not interested in finding out what he knew, but only in discovering what he didn't know. Every child from the age of five on up understands this and views every test as a trap. If a test is a duel with an enemy who is out to do you in, any and all means of outweighing him are legitimate. Cheating seems to me a perfectly logical and necessary feature of the system we have created.

Tests penalize thinkers and favor clever guessers. The child who sees the profoundly complex dimensions of any question and is unable to come up with the quick, smart answer his teacher has in mind always loses out. Tests also encourage children to think that there are always right answers, when we know this is not true: in the sciences, answers change as rapidly as scientific progress provides new right answers, and in the arts and social sciences, right answers vary with the teacher. Tests suggest that to fail is not to make progress. The exact reverse is so; all human progress has involved the necessary failures that go with creative experimentation.

A psychiatrist, treating adolescents who are drowning in tests, commented to me, "Tests have become such big business, I'm surprised they haven't been taken over by the rackets!" Over 30 million school exams are printed each year. Over 100 million standardized grade and high school tests are given each year, plus 2 million college admission tests. There are 60 million students in school. If each takes twenty tests a year, that would amount to 1 billion, 200 million tests, and we all know children are being given more than twenty tests a year.

Except to relieve our anxiety and insecurity, why do we

need constantly to know what a child is learning? Can you imagine being tested all the time, as an adult, to see what you are learning? Is there any test that could properly measure what life teaches us?

A mother in the nursery school where I work said that her daughter was going to be given an I.Q. test before entrance into kindergarten. In all seriousness, and in a genuinely worried tone, she said, "I don't know what my husband and I will do if it turns out she's not as brilliant as we think she is."

Well, there are two alternatives; they can throw out the kid or throw out the test. They've lived with their daughter for five years; the test was given by a stranger in an hour. Chances are, they will do what most parents do— they will assume the test is the better judge.

How marvelous it would be if, instead of providing a lousy education accompanied by thousands of meaningless tests, we tried providing a magnificent education and forgot about the tests! It's just barely possible that it is part of nature's plan for children to grow and learn—all they need is a decent place in which to do it, free from such impediments as tests.

Sex Education
in the Schools

I *do* believe in Santa Claus and the old-fashioned kind of fairies in the bottom of the garden—and I guess this tendency accounts for the fact that I even believed that America was ready for good sex education programs!

I couldn't have been more naïve. And now that I think about it, of course it was quite inevitable that despite the most careful planning by teams of absolutely topnotch educators, a wave of wild reaction has set in against sex education in the public schools.

Typical of this vocal nutty fringe is a letter I received, stating:

"I'm strictly opposed to sex education. Are we savages? Isn't there enough disease in the world? We have enough prostitution as it is. If we teach this garbage to children, God pity the next generation. If anyone tried to teach such trash to my child, he'd be jerked out of school immediately and I'd dare any dictator to force him back. God bless our flag.

About five years ago an organization came into being called SIECUS, the Sex Information and Education Council of the United States. It brought together many of the best and most experienced professionals in the field of sex and family life education and has attempted, with a good deal of success, to coordinate efforts to launch sex education programs. Long before this, however, there were many pilot projects being developed in many places.

Let me just mention two examples of communities that I know something about firsthand. Starting in the 1940's, the Association For Family Living began conducting sex education programs in the Chicago area on a voluntary basis. Parents met together first, then continued to meet for several sessions to discuss sex education so that the classes and home would be working together as a team. The program for the children met during nonschool hours and only children with written permission from parents were allowed to attend. The leaders of these groups were specially trained educators, social workers, psychologists, and psychiatrists who met in training seminars before and during their teaching assignments. Partly as a result of this pioneering work, as the time approached for these programs to become incorporated into the public school curriculum, Scott, Foresman and Company, a Chicago-based textbook house, published one of the very best sex education books* for school-age children. Today, in spite of all those years of careful planning and testing and evaluating, and in spite of the ultimate development of an outstanding program, Chicago has been beseiged by rabblerousing reactionaries who may very possibly destroy in a few months an excellent program built over a period of twenty to thirty years.

Much of the same thing is happening much closer to home on Long Island. Starting in the 1950's, Rockville Center was an example of another enlightened community developing an approach to sex education. Their voluntary

* *The Human Story* by Sadie Hofstein, 1967.

Saturday morning classes brought together more skilled and dedicated teachers and a more outstanding program than any I have known about personally. One would have thought that with such good experiences and leadership this would have been a suitable environment in which to begin introducing sex education in the public school curriculum—after all, a great many people were already well aware of the potential value of such programs. However, the hysterical fringe has been so effective in this area that the New York State Legislature has been designing a number of bills to kill sex education in the public schools.

Anyone who thinks that children are not getting sex education whether we provide it formally or not is even more naïve than those of us who believe in Santa Claus! By the time our children are ten or twelve, the information they have is extensive, often bizarre and incorrect, but exceedingly colorful and sophisticated.

A recent book called *Teach Us What We Want To Know** is based on a study of 5,000 Connecticut school children from kindergarten to twelfth grade. It is a fascinating report on today's kids—and an eye-opener on their candor and sophistication; they hear *everything* and want desperately to know the facts.

Sex education is a difficult and serious matter. There *are* realistic pitfalls and perfectly valid and wise demands for caution. What I am concerned with at the moment is the danger that a program that is desperately needed will be wiped out because of a vocal minority of screwballs.

If we learned anything from Sigmund Freud, it was surely that the sexually repressed, frustrated, and frightened tend to be the worst bigots around. They frequently work out some of their sex hang-ups by looking for communists under every bed—but what a field day they are going to have now that they can vent their miseries on finding communists *in* every bed! No more random targets for their sexual difficulties—now they can attack enlightened attitudes toward sex directly!

It would be funny if it were not also terrifying and disheartening. In a world as complex and difficult as this, our children need every kind of help we can give them to grow to healthy sexual maturity. Certainly good sex and family-life education courses are at least a step in the right direction. It is a terrible thing to see them being

* New York: The Mental Health Materials Center.

destroyed by the very people who needed them most when they were kids.

This is not meant to suggest that sex and family life education are easy subjects to introduce into the schools; there *are* very real hazards. There have been many poorly devised programs; there have been situations in which poor judgment was used and where the teaching staff has been inadequate to the task. When sex education has been irresponsibly or insensitively introduced, community concern is perfectly justifiable.

Sex and family life education deal with profound and powerful aspects of our lives. It is clear that sex information per se is not a satisfactory goal—what is needed is a sex education program that is a training ground for marriage and parenthood, and these are areas loaded with feelings and personal values. To plan genuinely helpful programs is an enormous challenge.

That we must have such programs, no matter how difficult the challenge, seems to me self-evident. The world and our lives have become too complicated—we are too crowded together on this planet, we are too interdependent, and the consequences can be too serious if we attempt to leave this task to individual families. The ones who scream the loudest against such programs are almost invariably those who are doing the least about it—or the most damage when they do it. There isn't a high-school-age youngster in this country who isn't being exposed to sex in one way or another. At present we permit his exposure to pornography, to all kinds of misinformation, to some of the most obscene, sexually oriented advertising—and yet say we don't believe in sex education. What we mean is that we are willing for children to get their sex education haphazardly but are not willing to take responsibility for this aspect of child guidance.

We cannot continue to back away from this issue; the stakes are too high. We have all the information we could require about the fact that the way a person feels about his own sexuality can greatly influence his social behavior—leading him toward a responsible and stable life or, at the other end of the scale, to serious and dangerous antisocial behavior, including the assassination of a President. It seems to me that nothing could be of more importance in the raising of our children than to do everything we can to help them develop sound attitudes about themselves as males and females as they grow toward adulthood.

It was therefore quite a shock to read recently in *The New York Times* that some psychiatrists are adding fuel to the fire of those opposed to sex education. Surely these are people who ought to know better than to advocate silence just because discussion of the issues may have inherent dangers and hazards. For example, the *Times* article quotes one psychiatrist as saying that when a boy reaches puberty, he has so many fears of castration that it is the wrong time for him to learn about eunuchs. I would think psychiatrists would be the first to acknowledge that at *any* stage of development a child's fantasies about such matters are likely to be ten times worse than any fact he may hear—that human irrationality is such that any truth tends to be less frightening and confusing than one's own imaginings.

It is perfectly true that teachers of sex and family life education must have special training; they must be prepared to provide not only a body of facts, but to develop attitudes toward these facts—self-understanding and understanding of relationships with others. They must have a profound understanding of child development and great skill in leading discussions. It's a tall order. It demands the best in us, and those who have special skills, such as psychiatrists, ought to be complaining less and helping more. There is no doubt that there are serious pitfalls, but that doesn't mean we can abdicate from the responsibility of creating the best programs we can.

One of the greatest fears among even the most enlightened parents is that sex education programs will introduce their children to ideas for which they are not yet ready. This is rarely true—but even if it were, we ought to take comfort from the fact that children simply do not pay any attention to ideas or facts that do not make sense to them. Whenever I get nervous about a child's exposure to sophisticated ideas, I remember that when I saw "It Happened One Night" with Claudette Colbert and Clark Gable I thought that the reason the man stopped the car to pick up the hitchhikers was because he was afraid of running over Claudette Colbert's foot. I wasn't retarded—just too young to know that men could be interested in ladies' legs. The best safeguard any child has against confusion or over-stimulation is the limits of his own life experience.